Who

DUE

WHO ARE YOU?

By the Same Author

DOLLARS AND SENSE

YOUR SILENT LANGUAGE

Elizabeth McGough

WHO ARE YOU?

A Teen-Ager's Guide
to Self-Understanding

illustrated by Tom Huffman

William Morrow and Company
New York 1976

Printed in the United States of America.

1 2 3 4 5 6 7 8 9 10

Library of Congress Cataloging in Publication Data

McGough, Elizabeth.
  Who are you?

  SUMMARY: Discusses some of the problems and changes of ado-lescence such as identity, peer pressure, school grades, family relation-ships, dating, decisions, and values.
  1. Adolescent psychology—Juvenile literature.
[1. Adolescence. 2. Psychology] I. Huffman, Tom. II. Title.
BF724.M255   155.5   76-41165
ISBN 0-688-22091-6
ISBN 0-688-32091-0 lib. bdg.

Contents

WHO ARE YOU?

Introduction

*Fortunately psychoanalysis is not the only way
to resolve inner conflicts.
Life itself still remains a very effective therapist.*
KAREN HORNEY

Just as a fuzzy caterpillar becomes a radiant butterfly, you become an adolescent by the dramatic metamorphosis of your body. But more than the obvious physical changes are taking place in your life. A major task for you as an adolescent is a reevaluation of yourself, a reworking of your identity. That sounds like a pretty big job—and, in fact, it is.

9

Adolescence has been described as "the wonder of leaving behind old patterns with their old feelings—and entering the new." During this period from youth to maturity you face some real challenges and many choices. You move rapidly toward true independence from your family. You learn to relate successfully to the opposite sex. You prepare for an occupation. You establish some values, your own philosophy of life.

Here is a book about you and for you. A number of teen-agers were willing to share private thoughts, their hopes, fears, and dreams with me. Drawing on their sharings I have tried to present a broad picture of the journey that occurs in adolescence. It is, I think, a remarkable trip from childhood to adulthood—full of sadness and joy, conflict and change.

Conflicts with parents, society, and oneself are a normal part of moving toward maturity, of finding a self-identity you carry through life. Now is the time when you begin to get an angle on who you are. You establish your personality through mistakes and testing, through shifting around your attitudes and values. You try different roles to see what fits, almost as though you are playacting.

The parent-child relationship faces some drastic changes. In a few years you move from being protected by and dependent upon your parents to a position of affectionate equal, responsible for your own actions and able to support yourself.

Changes and conflict are part of life, and they won't automatically disappear when you become an adult. But at no other time of life will you take such giant steps in personal growth. These are the years when you can learn to put yourself in charge, to make conscious decisions for what happens in your life. When you look in the mirror, you want to be able to say, "I like what I see. This is of my own making." You are accountable for what you do with your life.

A close look at the major changes and choices of adolescence may help you put yourself in control, as you journey in the search for self-identity to determine who you will be.

CHAPTER ONE

The Changing You

There is nothing permanent except change.
HERACLITIS

Have you ever wondered, "Who am I? What am I good for? What am I worth?" Psychologists tell us that finding our identity is one vital part of personality growth. Although your personality has been developing all through life, it has a special time of growth spurt, too, that coincides with your maturing body and expanding mind during adolescence. Physical changes can conspicuously affect personality development.

Dramatic Physical Changes

Adolescence begins biologically, and sexual development is a major theme. Hormonal changes begin to affect the body as you enter the phase of development called puberty. Germ cells are then produced by the reproductive glands, the testicles in boys and ovaries in girls.

The first menstruation signals sexual maturity for girls. For boys signs are not so sharply defined, although body growth rate changes and the sex organs grow nearly to adult size.

First menstruation, called menarche, happens normally between ages ten and seventeen—a wide variation, yet all in the normal range. About 70 percent of females have their first menstrual period at twelve, thirteen, or fourteen.

Girls may react to their first menstrual period with a range of feelings from joy to fear and shock. If a girl is unprepared and uninformed about this normal stage of development, she may be shocked. She may be anxious about her ability to accept her role as a woman or about feelings of sexuality. Many girls, though, are pleased and proud. The way you react to your developing body reflects many factors besides the physical changes alone.

Even before the first menstruation, breasts have enlarged almost to their mature stage. Development from bud stage to mature size takes about three years for most females. As girls enter a period of maximum body growth, the body takes on the graceful figure of a woman. Boys grow taller, and they develop the strength and body structures of a man. The face grows, too, as the head becomes longer and wider, sometimes enough to make the eyes look smaller and closer together than before. The nose and lower jaw grow more than other parts of the face, as proportions change from child features to adult features.

Brett, thirteen, was embarrassed by his rapidly growing nose, which seemed to overwhelm his face. He considered asking his parents to take him to a plastic surgeon to have it made smaller. He overheard his grandmother say, "I wouldn't have recognized Brett, his face has changed so much in two years." Positive that she meant his nose, Brett began to turn his face away when he talked to anyone.

Then his doctor pointed out, "We don't grow uniformly, as though you are blowing up a balloon that keeps the same proportions all along the way. We spurt now in one part of growth, and months later in another. We often look very different in a short time from our former appearance." Before Brett turned fifteen his jawline and other facial features had caught up with his nose growth, and he no longer worried about it.

Both boys and girls (and sometimes their parents) worry as their feet grow rapidly in early adolescence. This growth happens when the height spurt begins or just before it. Especially when it comes before or early in the height spurt, the feet may seem all out of proportion to the rest of the body. I once overheard someone at a junior-high baseball game say,

"No wonder he can't run those base paths faster. Those baseball shoes look like clown feet. They must be two sizes too
big!" The ballplayer in question had not grown much taller;
his feet were just a little ahead of the rest of him, which made
him appear awkward.

Facial and axillary (underarm) hair may also cause concern
or embarrassment. Some boys are uncomfortable when down
on the upper lip grows longer, coarser, and darker. Others
squirm when a parent says, "Say, don't you think you should
shave that fuzz off?" They may wish to wear the light mus-
tache as a badge of physical maturity. The external changes
that signal physical maturing are apt in themselves to create

stress in the lives of teen-agers. Perhaps just by knowing how normal the sequence of these events is may help you to deal with the inevitable body changes of adolescence.

What's Normal?

In *The Psychological World of the Teenager* Dr. Daniel Offer tells about an extensive study of average teen-age boys. Dr. Offer found that the boys had received very little sex education. Almost no help came from the adult world. Generally sex education amounted to situations much like this one: After a movie shown in school about insects mating, the athletic director asked if anyone had any questions. One boy asked a question about girls, and the class roared. That was the end of the question period. Then the boy's father took him aside at his mother's request. The father said, "You know all about girls, don't you?" The boy answered, "Sure, Dad," and that completed the sex education. "Everyone was passing the buck," the boy complained.

At the Center for Youth Development and Research in Minneapolis, Minnesota, Director Gisela Konopka stated that although young people speak very freely of sex, "parents and schools still shy away from sex information that is open, understandable and given before the onset of puberty." She said, "It seems unbelievable that in 1974 we still find quite a number of girls who did not know anything about menstruation before it occurred."

Since sex is seldom talked about openly and factually in most families, young people perceive a double meaning—sex is both evil and desirable. Unlike primitive cultures, where the young are not taught things they must later unlearn to get along in the adult world, parents may teach children that sex is wicked or secretive, then later expect the child to turn around and "adjust" without guilt to a normal sex life as a healthy adult. A fundamental in primitive society is that when the young are given adult privileges, they are then expected to assume adult responsibilities. In our society, the lines are not so clearly drawn.

While this chapter is not intended to give you a quick course in sex education, you can see that if you need accurate information about sex and reproduction, you are not alone. Here are several books that may be of interest to you:

Johnson, Eric W. and Corinne B. Johnson. *Love and Sex and Growing Up.* New York: Lippincott, 1970.

Johnson, Eric W. *Love and Sex in Plain Language.* New York: Lippincott, 1974; Bantam, 1974.

Johnson, Eric W. *Sex: Telling It Straight.* New York: Lippincott, 1970; Bantam, 1971.

Power, Jules. *How Life Begins.* New York: Simon and Schuster, 1965.

How do you feel about your body? Physical appearance is an important concern to most teen-agers. Many look in the mirror and wish for something different from what they see.

While girls tend to worry more about their body than boys, both usually have a more negative view of their physical appearance than others do. Beauty has different definitions in various ages and cultures. In flapper days it was fashionable to be flat chested. Judging from current popular media in the United States, large breast size is of great interest and some importance today. Girls focus on bust development and sometimes fall prey to ads that guarantee to increase the breast size. Fourteen-year-old Michelle wrote to an advice columnist: "There must be hundreds of girls just like me waiting for an answer to this: I'm flat chested. What can I do? And don't tell me to wear a padded bra. I've considered sending for creams and bust developers, but I don't see how these can do any good. You must get hundreds of letters asking this." The answer, in essence, was: When all is said and done, you have to make the best of what you have. Many models are flat chested. Give yourself a year or two to see if you still care so much. It may not seem quite so important. In the meantime, do wear a padded bra and don't slouch. Self-confidence in other facets of life may help you overcome what you feel lacking in your figure. True enough, you may never rate the wide eyes on the beach that bosomy Barbie does—so how about being tops in something else?

Brian at fourteen had the physical appearance of many twelve-year-old boys. "Well, at least I don't have to pay full price at the movies," he said, reaching for the barbells he worked out with daily as he tried to develop a supermasculine frame. Boys sometimes think the size of their genital organs is an indication of their manliness or of their ability to find sexual satisfaction as an adult. Researchers William H. Masters and Virginia E. Johnson say both these ideas are myths and have no scientific basis.

Early and Late Maturing

No one wants to be too different from his peers, especially at a time when one's identity is changing rapidly. A school psychologist told the story of Nancy, who went to see him for a fairly common reason. She would do anything not to have to take a shower in PE. She used every excuse imaginable and had even forged notes from her parents asking that she be excused from that class. She was an extreme case. Yet many young teen-agers go through much the same subterfuge for the same reason. They can't face having their body seen, for their maturity timetable doesn't seem up to standard in their opinion. Early maturers among girls sometimes are embarrassed to be too full-bosomed while their classmates are still little girls. Sixth-grade girls prefer to be in the same developmental stage as their own age group. Later they seem comfortable to be developing faster than their friends. In contrast, early maturing boys generally enjoy the advantages of being treated more positively, more like an adult than late maturers.

Unfortunately, while we have control over some physical features—such as hair coloring or teeth straightening—the genetic factors that largely determine maturing can't be influenced by our wishes. According to recent studies of maturity, each maturity pattern has certain advantages in adulthood. Early maturing boys were rated above average in physical attractiveness, since our culture tends to emphasize masculinity even above handsomeness. In a scientific study that contrasted behavior, experiences, and attitudes of both early- and late-maturing boys, those who matured early were often student leaders, successful and relaxed, without the need to push for status. They had self-confidence, were socially capable, and independent. Late maturers were often treated as little boys longer and were rated as less attractive. These boys had lower confidence levels and sometimes felt rejected and inadequate. They rebelled against their parents more. However, these younger-looking boys, at a disadvantage because of smaller size, surpassed early maturers in eagerness, initiative, and sociability. They learned how to compensate. In follow-up studies in adulthood, they were still eager and innovative. They were rated independent and insightful. Early maturers continued to be poised and responsible, comfortable in social roles. Boys maturing at the average age developed much like early maturers.

Similar studies of girls' maturation patterns found similar, but less dramatic, results. Any such study does not, of course, conclude that every person who matures late has personality traits that tend toward a negative self-concept, any more than one could say that all early maturers are relaxed and confident.

There is good sense in the well-known adage, "Try to accept

what you cannot change." Self-acceptance is a stumbling block everyone faces, whether as an adolescent or as an adult.

Sex Identity

As you develop a sense of identity, you also develop the pattern of behavior our culture accepts as appropriate to your sex. Sex roles are partly learned in early childhood, when, until recently anyway, little girls play house and little boys pretend they are daddies and go off to work each day. These stereotypes are changing slowly.

Girls would rather be boys, right? Wrong! The idea of the *completely* dependent, pliant follower of the male is a myth created by constant repetition. She has rarely actually existed in this country. However, women in our culture are becoming more self-confident and freer to decide on a variety of roles in life. They no longer feel that wife and mother are the only roles they will fill, although a majority still expect them to be a part of their future. Most girls expect to have a job or career after high school or college. They expect marriage to be a partnership, not to be ruled by the male. They think husbands should help with chores and children, just as they expect to help with finances of the family. They expect to continue growing after marriage.

According to American tradition, boys are aggressive. Researchers say that the adolescent boy knows and has known since childhood that he must achieve and produce. He recognizes that he must be a breadwinner both before and after he marries. Boys in our society are encouraged to be assertive and independent, not timid or passive. When he achieves this standard, say social scientists, he is usually self-confident, energetic, and well organized.

On the other hand, girls are traditionally supposed to be passive and to control aggressions. Girls should not compete openly with boys, either in sports or for scholastic honor. A girl may be tender and submissive, act more helpless or cry, while a boy must suffer in silence, rarely show his feelings except for anger. If a girl doesn't fit into the traditional female mold, she has to struggle with her feelings of wanting to do her own thing, perhaps at the risk of being isolated socially. Many women in their thirties and forties today admit to having a pretty unhappy time in their early twenties when it was far less acceptable for a woman to desire a career as well as or instead of marriage. Still, some girls today say they play dumb around boys because they think boys prefer them to be that way. Yet the comment beautiful but dumb can hardly be interpreted as a compliment.

Some families continue to set different standards for each sex. Parents are often more protective of a girl, in an attempt to care for her, which may actually deprive her of becoming a fulfilled, responsible adult. Jennie, at sixteen, is an example of one girl who found good reason to wish to be a boy. She resented her two brothers. "They get to have all the fun, go everywhere with my father—to ball games, hiking—and I get to stay home with my mother, who slaves over the house all day." While her brothers had few restrictions on their behavior and looked forward to seeing the world around them, her mother complained a lot and never seemed to enjoy life. Jennie's model of female life wasn't very appealing.

It has often been difficult to escape from society's pressures to conform to its ideal of masculine and feminine behavior. Yet today in the latter part of the twentieth century, society begins to recognize your right and responsibility to explore your potential. You accept yourself as a person first, then as a woman or a man. You need not succumb to a stereotype. If math and competitive sports are your forte, why not pursue your interests wholeheartedly, whether you are male or female? No one questions a boy who makes this choice. Do you think a girl should

be discouraged from competing with boys for scholastic honor and in sports?

With the flourishing of the women's liberation movement and other pressures to improve the status of women, the life-style of many women who contribute valuable services outside the family is no longer considered a contradiction to the feminine ideal. Such life-styles will likely influence future identity development in girls.

The once-ideal role for men is changing, too. As women achieve more freedom, masculine stereotypes are breaking down. A male need not be highly competitive, devoid of emotions, always in strict control as he earns a living. Men may also be relaxed, sympathetic, and involved in nurturant roles such as elementary- and nursery-school teachers or social workers. Today once-typical sex roles are no longer typical.

Take Inventory

In the search to discover yourself, you can begin by taking stock of what you have to work with. What do you like about yourself? What do you dislike most about yourself? Write out these personal feelings about yourself. What kind of person are you? How would you describe yourself? How would your friends describe you? Are you glad you're you? Would you rather be someone else? Here are some guidelines that may help you in self-assessment.

Ask yourself: What are my good points? Make a long list of

them. What do I do well? Am I better than other people at something? What things do I like to do? Make a list, with pluses and minuses, including all the things about yourself that bother you. Your list may look something like this:

PLUS

Like people
Fairly good grades
Can ski
Willing to work in a group
Best feature: green eyes
Loyal to friends
Good listener
Play the guitar and sing

MINUS

Don't like to speak up in class
Not a leader
Embarrass easily
Trouble talking to parents
Quick temper
Not comfortable with opposite sex
Need to lose ten pounds

Check off the things that bother you most. Then consider what can be done about them. Ask yourself, "Do I often feel inferior? If so, can I identify the circumstances that cause me to feel this way? Can I avoid these situations? What alternatives do I have?" You'll feel better for having faced the problems, and in the process you may solve some of them. Begin work on any major ones. See a counselor or talk with a friend, but don't just sit back and say, "Well, that's the way I am."

Our weaknesses have a way of clinging like parasites, while our strengths seem as fleeting as a butterfly in summer. But try taking stock of those strengths and putting them to work at changing the weaknesses. For example, being a good listener could indeed help when talking to parents. Underline the minus points that could be changed. You could join a group of both sexes in which you will have the chance to make some contribution. The interchange may help you be comfortable with the opposite sex. You could force yourself to speak up in class a few times on a subject you know well. Ask a question, or volunteer an answer. You may help your grades and begin to speak up more often in class.

Accept What's Past

A high-school student wrote for a composition assignment, "What I am today is my parents' fault. If I stay that way, it's my fault." Indeed, much of the way you feel about yourself and much of what you bring to the teen years reflects your child-hood. There's a story about jazz musician Duke Ellington that claims he was asked on a television talk show, "Can you recall some of the hard times you had before you became a success?"

"No, I can't," he said. "When I was a little boy, I was loved so much and held so much, I don't think my feet ever touched the ground until I was seven years old." Whatever our childhood was like, we should accept our past for what it was without blame and recriminations, however difficult that may be to do.

Look at the different attitudes of two toddlers, Lisa and Ellen. Ellen, second child in the family, was a fussy baby and was often left to "just cry it out." Her parents did not believe in babying a child, and she was left alone in her playpen while her mother took care of the house. Ellen was very jealous of a new brother, born before she was three. Ellen thinks the world offers little comfort and security. Lisa, on the other hand, has a special place in her family, for she is the youngest of four children. A vigorous, active child, Lisa loves to play with blocks, clay, and paints; she enjoys following her mother around, imitating her. In turn, her mother enjoys the experience of having a little girl. Lisa likes people and trusts them. They have met her childhood needs well. Lisa and Ellen have very different concepts of their environment and of their ability to cope with it.

All of us resist change, even when we know we should change behavior. Most of such resistance is the result of childhood experiences. The more insecure we are, the more we feel afraid to change. Change means moving into the unknown, meeting all the "what ifs" you can possibly imagine. If you recognize this universal tendency, you may then be able to say, "I don't have to feel and behave the way I did when someone made all the decisions for me. I'm no longer a child, and I can accept or reject things." And, in fact, in adolescence new cognitive, or intellectual, growth allows you to think differently from the way you did as a young child. You begin to see more than one side of things, and you can think in the abstract. Moral development goes hand in hand with new intellectual abilities, too. You begin to question adults who say one thing and do another. You also examine your own code of behavior to evaluate the moral lessons you learned as a child.

If you know your body and your feelings, your likes, dislikes, strengths, and weaknesses, you can begin to accept yourself— who you are, what you are, and where you are at this special moment. Knowing yourself does not mean doing nothing about your shortcomings. But it does imply that you know what you have to work with. You can say, "Here I am. Now let's go from there."

Psychologists say that of all the later stages of life after childhood, adolescence is the time when the most profound changes of personality can occur. Adolescence can provide a second chance. You can undo damage done in childhood, heal any wounds of parental inconsistency or ignorance, move beyond any handicaps you may have had to find and develop your potential.

Psychoanalyst Sigmund Freud was once asked, "What should a normal person be able to do well?" His answer was *lieben und arbeiten*, "love and work." He meant production of something meaningful balanced with the capacity to love, both in friendship and in sexual love.

CHAPTER TWO

Who Are You?

We do not deal much in facts
when we are contemplating ourselves.
MARK TWAIN

If you were asked, "Who are you?" how would you answer? You might say, "I'm a sophomore at Hanford High School, I'm student-council representative from my homeroom, and I belong to the Drama Club," and so on. We identify ourselves by the groups we belong to and the activities we participate in.

"In ninth grade you try on attitudes, interests, and even a whole personality for size to see what fits," said seventeen-year-old Christie. "You choose and reject before you find what is your own." Christie's experience was typical. Identity in the teens is tentative, experimental, and ever changing. Teens use their peers to help shape their beliefs, to weigh values, and to chisel out new conclusions.

Along with resolving sexual feelings, one of the central concerns that motivates teen-agers seems to be interpersonal power, finding acceptance with peers. Cliques and gangs play a major role in social development, with a social system that is easy to recognize in most schools.

Peers (age-mates) have even more influence at this age than they did during childhood. A few teen-agers stay outside the social swim by choice. They study, have hobbies or sports with one friend or sometimes on their own. A few others are rejected by their peers. They exist in isolation or with an occasional other lonely soul.

The Crowd, The Clique

You can be an insider or an outsider or somewhere in between. Social scientists who have evaluated teen social systems say when you get into a crowd, you've really arrived. You have achieved something important. The first stage of adolescent group development is a clique, something like a preadolescent gang. You have a group of friends of the same sex who do things together and who have similar attitudes and opinions. Clique members may be petty and intolerant of anyone outside their group. They may exclude others of different abilities, race, religion, or different dress and appearance. This first clique is about the size of the family, with members all from the same social background. They are also alike in experience and interests.

To be a true member, you have to show that you are ready to conform to group values and authority. Cliques are often neighborhood oriented, and pairs of best friends belong to the same clique. Girls seem to need close friendships more than

boys do. Girls also place more status value on belonging to the right clique. They may scheme and dream up certain ways to show they are different from other groups in dress or speech or behavior. For example, all of Jennie's clique may sport an Afro hair style one day of the week. They announce, "Hey, look at us. We're a solid group apart from the rest of you."

Later in adolescence cliques form larger groups, the crowd. Within each crowd are cliques of both sexes, where leaders and status exist, even though group members may deny a pecking order, or status hierarchy. How does one person get to be the leader? Through a combination of factors, ranging from personality traits to having some material item such as a car, money, or access to a place for group activity. This pecking order fluctuates. Any leader may fall out of favor if he doesn't act the way the group expects.

Cliques and crowds serve different functions. Clique activity centers around talking, getting ready for crowd activities. Clique members pass out information about crowd functions and evaluate them afterward. The crowd centers on large social activities, parties and dances. The crowd is much like a reservoir of acceptable friends. A new member in a crowd has to conform initially, once he has pushed his way in. One teen-ager says, "If you get in and push yourself, you get in the easiest. If you stand back, you won't make it." However, if you think you're a wheel, superior, you get cut down to size fast. If you keep this attitude, you will be shoved out. In many crowds, how you rate with the opposite sex measures your status.

Identity, Finding You

Whether you belong to a specific group or not, your life is affected by groups. Being included may offer advantages, or being excluded may have disadvantages. While there is the danger of being enslaved by your peers, there are also developmental hazards in being isolated. Being involved in a peer group is part of life. Here are some of the things you accomplish through peer association:

▶ A way to learn group participation, a prelude to job involvement. If you are always a sheep and let everyone decide for you, chances are your job involvement may continue in the same pattern. Someone will tell you what to do, and you will follow. You won't seek new ways to solve problems.

▶ Interpersonal competence. You test your social capabilities in an open arena. You try your range of power to affect others. You learn to give and take, to make others feel accepted, and to manage even unfriendly or hostile situations. Peer society is a natural way of encouraging good relationships with same-sex and opposite-sex friends.

▶ A source of rich, widely varied information about your environment. You learn about other families, values, crowds, cliques, and how group actions differ from an individual's.

▶ Security. You find security in being with others whose needs are similar to yours and who are experiencing adolescence at the same time that you are. They know how it is.

▶ Strength and encouragement. The strength and support

of a group can help you accomplish things you could not do alone.

► Stimulation, both agreeable and disagreeable. Being with others helps stimulate your feelings and your mind. You maintain a higher level of achievement through the social structure of peer groups.

► Some standards and an external source of control. According to Peter Blos, who has studied adolescence, teen-agers immerse themselves in the peer group and accept its standards as "infallible and regulatory." This behavior helps you move away from the family, yet gives you some standards to go by. If you cling to dependency on peers long after the need for it has passed, development is foreclosed or blocked. Real self-regulation and independence is then not within your grasp. Dependence on peers increases in late childhood, peaks in early adolescence, and actually decreases in later adolescence.

► An identity separate from your family. The slang you use identifies you as distinct from adults. You want to feel the strength of a group, yet be apart from the family. Girls wear standardized hair styles and shades of lipstick and nail polish. If these fashions are adopted by adults, they change quickly.

► Appropriate sex-role behavior. The sex role learned at home and in childhood is strengthened. Peer acceptance hinges on appropriate sex-typed behavior. For example, the accepted female role may be having the reputation of being fun and showing characteristics of warmth, consideration for others, and social skills. An accepted boy might be expected to stand up against an attack and to have athletic skills.

▶ Perspective. Learning how others see you helps you get to know yourself.

During the reshuffling of identity in adolescence, feelings of insecurity are common. You may crave group acceptance more than ever. Herd values are important for a few years until your own image comes into focus. Adolescent peer power is neither good nor bad; it's simply there. As you seek independence, hacking to free yourself from parental shackles, you may think your parents belong back in the Stone Age and that they can't possibly understand. Try as they may to do so, they are not teen-agers now, and they are not having the same problems that you are. As fourteen-year-old Jana said, "Parents still see us as little kids." It becomes important to share your private matters with someone outside the family, someone who is developmentally right where you are and who is not emotionally involved.

Peer Power

Suppose someone showed you and nine friends three cards that showed three lines varying in length. You were asked to raise your hand when a card with the longest line was held up. One line was obviously longer. The comparison was easy to make. The medium-length line was shown. All your friends raised their hands. What would you do?

This exact experiment has been done many times. The tenth

person usually has a puzzled expression, looks around the room in surprise, then shrugs and raises his hand too. The other nine are confederates of the tester. The tenth person can easily see the others are wrong, but he cannot quite force himself to say, "Hey, you're all wrong." In these experiments done by S. E. Asch, he found that group pressure greatly distorted judgment. More than 35 percent of subjects conformed, would not call the lines as they saw them. Do you remember the story of "The Emperor's New Clothes"?

A certain amount of conformity to group standards is essential to get along in the world. Conformity to rules is needed to make traffic regulation work well. So you learn to conform early in life.

But by blindly conforming in the face of your own judgment you risk your sense of identity. Jean told this story: "Once in a while the group just decides to pick on someone. Maybe they're jealous of her. One time they started picking on Donna, took her towel in the showers after PE, hid her clothes, and 'accidentally' dropped her sweater on the wet floor. I couldn't believe they could be so mean. But I didn't do anything. In fact, I was part of it for a while." A conformist doesn't stop to think about someone's feelings. Jean allowed the clique's power to keep her from speaking up. When you are too dependent on the crowd, you can miss out on questioning and thinking through matters that make you a stronger individual.

Everyone at times is afraid to assert himself for fear of ridicule. First he conforms in small things, and maybe later in more important ones. Brett wasn't happy with himself for shoplifting just because all his pals did. Laura, in spite of her own convictions, found things got out of control with her boyfriend because she didn't want to lose him—and, after all, wasn't everyone doing it? Like Laura and Brett, many try so hard to be accepted that they do things they don't truly believe in. Here are a few places to start if you'd like to make some changes:

▶ Don't be a puppet, with your peers pulling the strings. A conformist waits to hear what everyone has to say, then follows the crowd. After a while you lose your initiative, no longer have the courage to do things on your own.

▶ Stop! Take a careful look at your activities. What do you do that is really to impress or please someone else? What do you do because you genuinely want to?

Jeff, sixteen, said, "In junior high I never thought I had anything going for me. You get peer pressure everywhere you turn—the way you walk, the way you handle yourself. When you let Joe down the block make all the decisions for you, you get down on yourself. Then I realized that if I wasn't for myself, if I didn't find other things that would make me happy, no one would. You can wind up going out drinking or to a party every Saturday when you'd rather go to a movie."

Everyone needs to feel satisfied, to have his individual needs met. Don't hide your taste for symphonies because your friends think it's weird. If you hate roller-skating, find a graceful way to say you're not going. Life becomes dull and frustrating when your own needs are always cast aside for what other people say you ought to do or like.

▶ You'll never please everyone, so expect a few enemies. If you think everyone likes you, you've probably stayed in the background, never spoken out much. Don't, of course, go out of your way to antagonize someone. But think of someone who has no enemies. Are they too sweet to be true, a bit phoney? Who wants to be bland? If you've never cared enough about anything, never felt strongly enough to argue a point, then maybe you have no enemies, but perhaps you feel that people don't take much notice of you either.

▶ When you don't agree, walk away. Peer pressure can be

stifling. A group of seniors were reflecting upon earlier years. Steve said, "When I first came here, the kids I hung around with cut classes. My own feelings were, Why? I didn't tell them off or cut them out. I didn't stop being friends, but it was not the same. You have to let people know that no matter what they do, you'll do what's right for you. No need to be an outcast, but you see that some friendships can change."

Karen said, "When you don't conform they wonder what's wrong. If you don't neck at parties, they say, 'Do you think you're better than we are?' It's hard to tell yourself that, after all, pleasing yourself is more important. But you have to live with yourself."

Other seniors said they thought that no one should stay in one crowd too long, that they should try different behavior and attitudes.

▶ Everyone has limitations. Our society may lead you to feel that everyone has to be a superstar, a top tennis player, a fashion model, brilliant and accomplished, loved by everyone. Sound ridiculous? Of course! Yet many people compare themselves to the top in everything and feel unhappy. David talked about maturity. "A lot of us are trying to be somebody else—a famous actor or athlete, without the same talent or environment they had. It's more important to be who you are, do what you can do well. I've decided to accept my limitations and go with what I have."

Psychologist Jess Lair summed it all up when he wrote, "I ain't much, baby, but I'm all I've got."

Negative Status Symbols

Sometimes when all they've got doesn't seem like quite enough, people use negative identity to get recognition. If you can't be a good example, why not be a bad example rather than a nonentity. Here is one of many tape-recorded conversations I had with teen-agers.

Interviewer: What is the hardest thing to do on your own in your school?

Scott, fifteen: You get a lot of pressure to goof off. If you try to get good grades, you're weird. You're not cool. You're too willing to go along with the establishment. I was even asked, "Is that all you've got to do?"

Sandi, eighteen: There's more pressure when you are a sophomore. If you can just ride it out and stay your own person, you'll be okay. But if you get in the wrong crowd, or in the rut of giving in to pressure, you can mess yourself up a lot by the time you're a senior. Generally things start to mellow out by the end of the junior year. You can wind up with a label you'd like to shake if you are an easy mark for every new fad.

Interviewer: What do you mean, every new fad?

Sandi: Right now the big status symbol is to have older boyfriends. Everyone asks, "How old is your boyfriend?" You answer, "Nineteen." They say, "Mine's twenty-three." A real triumph. A lot of things you just have to shrug off, calmly do your own thing. Quietly.

Scott: I agree that it's harder when you're younger. You get a lot of pressure to drink at dances.

Interviewer: Do you see negative identity?

Scott: You bet! Billy, a kid on my street, for example. The highlight of his career was getting kicked out of school for drinking in eighth grade. He showed up the next week with a grin from ear to ear. That was really class. It gave him status. He wasn't a chicken. Some other kids got in trouble for stealing, breaking into a country club. They were really wheels for a while. Hard to see why, but they were. I guess they didn't have anything to stand out for, anything to be in the spotlight about. And suddenly, like someone who takes a shot at the president, they get a little fame. I admit I felt jealous that they should be treated the way they were, but I sure didn't want to get my kicks the way they did. I figure they have to live that one down for a long time.

Jennie, eighteen: I think most kids start drinking the way I did, too, with a good push from your friends. Everybody in my crowd did, and it made me feel good. My parents didn't know I drank because I never drank at home. I started on New Year's Eve when I was fourteen. I only drank beer at first—and I didn't think you could be an alcoholic on beer. After a while I didn't know which was more miserable—being drunk or being sober.

Scott: Sometimes when you see so many of your friends drinking and really having a blast, you think, well, why not? Then when you see the same kids making a fool of themselves, sick, drunk, you don't think they're so smart after all. Four varsity players got kicked off the basketball team for drinking. You have to decide for yourself if drinking is worth the risk.

Sandi: A lot of times a party is nothing but everybody trying out something and pushing you to do it, too. It can be smoking, drinking, or drugs. Maybe you try it and that's the end of it. But if it makes you feel big, and you really need something to prop you up right now, you might get started with something on a regular basis.

Scott: I'll go along with that. A lot of us try marijuana and that's the end of it. It's curiosity and group pressure. Some of us do it to defy adults. But some get on to drugs because they can't handle their own life. They can be lonely, really down, and drugs help ease the pain.

Jennie: I finally went to Alcoholics Anonymous with a friend who belonged to Alateen, for kids who have an alcoholic parent. I learned a lot about myself. I don't know why other kids drink, but I know that at first it did make my life easier. It made me feel bigger, more important than I really was. And it's so available. I mean, you can get booze everywhere. Everybody approves of drinking. Nobody approves of heroin or LSD. Even my friends' parents gave me drinks.

Scott: That's true, our society does approve of drinking—but not to the point that you can't live without it. Or that it runs your life.

As one student commented, "You've got to stay your own person." If you can, then there's a warm sense of security when you are with people who face the same problems, behave the same way you do, and wear the same fashions—symbols of belonging. Everyone is trying out a variety of roles, wondering what kind of person he or she wants to be. Standing together with your own generation feels good. In the crowd you don't seem to be alone anymore.

CHAPTER THREE

Self-Esteem

It may be called the Master Passion,
the hunger for self-approval.
MARK TWAIN

Self-esteem affects every possible aspect of behavior, motivation, ability to learn, capacity to grow and change, choice of friends, mates, and careers. It is probably not an exaggeration to say that a strong, positive self-image could be the best possible preparation for a successful life.

All the things you prize, or value, affect your self-esteem.

If a quality is not important to you, the fact that you don't have it won't shatter your self-esteem. For example, suppose you took a test and found that you rated very low on mechanical ability. You know you are not mechanically inclined and don't care about it, so you shrug your shoulders and say, "What else is new?" Your self-esteem is not damaged. According to psychologist William James, "Our self-feeling in this world depends entirely on what we *back* ourselves to be and do." The gap between your aspirations, what you'd like to be, and your actual performance results in poor self-appraisal.

The important factors in development of self-esteem are:

▶ The amount of respect, acceptance, and concerned treatment you receive from *significant* others in your life.

▶ Your history of success and the status you have in the world.

▶ Your values and goals—you judge your success, the power you have, and the attention you receive from others in view of your values and goals.

▶ The way you respond to devaluation. You may attach no importance to someone's judgment of you.

You make yourself feel worthy to live by making yourself competent. If you do things without thinking or reasoning, then become angry and disgusted with yourself, you undercut your competence. You then lose your sense of worthiness. Have you ever said, "I don't know why I did that. I guess I just didn't think."? You judge yourself by some standard, consciously or unconsciously; you want to be right. To be right makes you feel good. To be wrong threatens pain, disapproval.

Consider what happens when you make somebody feel bad. You nit-pick, put your brother down to make yourself feel big for the moment. But chances are you don't really feel good about it afterwards. Most people know their deepest selves, even when they'd like to hide their motives. Self-confidence and self-respect are inseparable.

A person may be competent in his job, yet may not feel successful if he doesn't think his job is important. A student may be a good scholar, but still form a negative self-concept if he doesn't have attention and acceptance from his peers.

Psychologist Stanley Coopersmith made an intensive study of self-esteem to determine conditions that contribute to positive or negative self-feelings. He agreed with other researchers who felt that ethnic or social background has little to do with our self-esteem. Students were asked to check whether each statement described how he usually felt, either Like Me, or Unlike Me. Here are a few of his statements:

I often wish I were someone else.
I get easily upset at home.
I'm pretty happy.
I wish I were younger.
It's pretty tough to be me.
Kids pick on me very often.

Things usually don't bother me.

Kids usually follow my ideas.

I'm doing the best work I can.

I spend a lot of time daydreaming.

How would you answer each of these? Your answers may give you a clue to your own self-esteem.

High or Low Self-Esteem

If you could tune in on the thoughts of someone with high self-esteem you might hear something like this: "I think I'm valuable and important, at least as good as other kids of my age and experience. People I care about respect me, and they consider my opinions. I can give my views without being afraid people will laugh. People respect and ask for my ideas, since I can usually defend my viewpoints. I trust my own judgment, and I think I have control over my own actions. I feel I can influence others. New and challenging tasks are a pleasure. I don't get all churned up when things don't go smoothly at first. I don't depend on somebody else to make up my mind for me. I generally put out good quality work, and I plan to do some worthwhile things in my life—and possibly great things."

A person with low self-esteem might sound like this: "I don't consider myself important and can't think of many reasons why anyone would especially like me. A lot of things I do don't work out very well. I usually think other people have better ideas. I'm not sure of my feelings and ideas, haven't thought much about goals. I more or less go along with the crowd. New experiences don't turn me on. I'd rather stick to familiar, safe ground. Often, even when I try my darndest, things don't pan out for me. I really don't expect to do anything great. I guess this is pretty much out of my control. I'll be happy if I can just get a job. I certainly don't expect anyone to seek my opinion on anything, and I don't blame them."

A person with medium self-esteem would have attitudes falling somewhere between these two. They would have some positive attitudes, but they would not be as strong as those of the high self-esteem person. If you have medium self-esteem, you generally see yourself more favorably than unfavorably. It has been said that people with high and low self-esteem live in markedly different worlds. Would you agree?

If we look at two girls, Ann and Jean, both fifteen, we get a sharp picture of high and low self-esteem. Both are intelligent, attractive. Ann believes in herself and Jean does not. In class Ann volunteers answers. Jean never answers unless she is asked. She is afraid others will have a negative reaction or laugh at her, so she keeps opinions to herself. At a beach picnic Ann plays volleyball, swims, dances. Jean sits on a blanket, has to be coaxed to play, which she does halfheartedly. She feels she has zero to offer. Her behavior makes others think she is aloof, cool, so they avoid her and in turn feed her conviction that she's not very important. She sees herself as a loser, expects to fail, and so she does. Jean is a perfect example of

the adage, "An image believed becomes a prophecy fulfilled."

Just as you feed your physical self, you also need to feed your psychological self. You must find ways to feed your self-esteem.

You join groups to be somebody and achieve identity. Then as identity grows stronger, you have courage to go alone if you wish. High self-esteem allows independent activity and exploring. People with low self-esteem join, but they are usually passive and do not offer opinions. Although sources of self-esteem vary with age, motivating factors stay the same. Babies want their mother's recognition; children, their parents';

teen-agers, their peers', parents', teachers', and other important adults'. Adults seek recognition in their communities, from their bosses, their spouses, their children.

A student with a low self-image has no interest in student government, much like a politically apathetic citizen. As Brian, a typical low self-esteemer put it, "I'm never sure enough of myself to be able to tell someone else what to do. And I don't want someone else bossing me either." He rarely competes, because there's always a chance he could fail. Or others could be angry if he does better than they do. If he fails, all the world can see how inadequate he is. People with low self-esteem are sure everyone's watching, waiting for them to fumble. They also have more illness symptoms, migraine headaches, depression, and loneliness.

Mark, a high SE teen-ager, says of competition: "It adds spice to your life, makes you work harder. If there's no competition, you just poke along, never improve. If I go out to play golf alone, I never play my best. But with a teammate, I really pour it on."*

A high SE person is better able to defend himself against threatening feelings of inadequacy. As demonstrated in the three-lines experiment, many people conform to avoid criticism. Stanley Coopersmith asked students, "If dissent would provoke criticism, would you say nothing?" While 82 percent of low SE students said yes, only 25 percent of the high SE group said they would not dissent. He also asked, "Would you say you make friends easier or harder than most people?" * Over 87 percent of the lows said they found it hard to make friends. People who see themselves as having trouble socially often evaluate themselves poorly no matter how poised they seem to others.

Self-image is not a constant, never-changing state. It's normal to feel down some of the time. Usually the mood is a fleeting feeling that you can overcome. But your overall feeling of worth—the knowledge deep in your heart you are an important being—is the key to behavior. A priest once counseled a woman when she felt very low, "Remember this: God made you, and God doesn't make junk." No matter what your religious beliefs, you can be encouraged by his simple statement.

Everyone occasionally faces depreciating comments from others. Juvenile counselors say they are amazed how low some teen-agers feel about themselves and that often families have unknowingly (but sometimes intentionally) caused this situation. Building oneself up after years of snubs and of feeling small and insignificant can be a monumental task. But the building blocks are there in everyone.

▶ Recognize that your worth does not depend on your every action—the result of a race, a project you do, or a grade on a test. A healthy person sees his self as separate from his acts. He can still be worthy of love, though not everything he does is admirable or acceptable.

▶ You matter just because you exist.

▶ Identify the situations that make you feel inferior. What can you do about them?

► Don't dwell on misfortunes. What you bring to this stage of life can't be helped. Concern yourself with what you carry from adolescence to adulthood.

► Seek people who treat you with respect. One hour of basking in positive reflections can make enormous changes in self-confidence. The way others treat you is your vision of the world.

► Anxiety and depression come to most of us at one time or another. Don't be ashamed when you feel this way.

► A feeling shared is a burden eased. Bearing pain in solitude is always worse than when you know that someone else is with you. This help does not mean the person is feeling sorry for you. It means sharing, caring, understanding or trying to understand without making judgments.

► Adapt. You can cope with feelings by action or a change in focus. Of course, you can also adapt by denial, isolation, or rationalization, but these are immature defenses.

► One of the best sources of confidence is *doing*. You won't gain confidence by staying put and blaming "circumstances." Go out and try.

Everyone needs to feel competent to manage his or her world. Feeling good about yourself is a building block for managing your life.

Everyone is rejected at some time in life and feels deserted, but the rejection needn't be the end of your world. Enrico

Caruso was once told that his voice sounded like wind howling through the window. Pianist Ignace Paderewski was told that his hands were too small to master the keyboard.

You can see that if you feel rejected sometimes, you are not alone. In a study of adolescent problems, the number one problem was "Myself," according to 800 students. They said being rejected, being popular, and emotional ups-and-downs gave them the most trouble.

Coping with Loneliness and Shyness

Emotional growth is often painful, but pain is not confined to adolescence. Mood swings make even a healthy adult feel lonely, empty, hopeless. With the intense mood swings of the teen years, you may feel as though all the troubles of the world descend on you at times. How you cope with the pains of these years can strengthen you for adulthood.

Loneliness is one of the pains that is especially demoralizing. Loneliness can drive people to alcoholism, drug abuse, and suicide. You can be lonely at a party when you feel you don't belong. Other people have someone who cares more about them than anyone cares about you. You can be lonely in a train station or on the school bus jammed full of kids. You need not be literally alone to feel lonely. In fact, experts say that loneliness may have little to do with what's going on around you but instead with what's going on inside you. When you feel lonely and can't seem to shake your misery, you worry that you aren't more popular. It hurts that no one notices you, asks you to join in, and no one seems to want to know you. And it's true, people are apt not to want to know someone who is only interested in him- or herself.

One way to combat loneliness is to get out of your self-involvement. If you are interested in life, in what's going on around you, people will be interested in you and care about you.

▶ Find what's good about yourself to like. Go back to your list of positive things about yourself. Work on the liabilities, one day at a time. Say, "Just for today, I'm going to like myself. Just for today, I'll not snack between meals, a beginning to shed those extra pounds I hate. Just for today, I'll smile at someone, say hello to someone I'd like to know. When the day is through, I'll be pleased with myself."

▶ Reach out to others. For one day at a time, try noticing someone else. Not a big, phoney act. Tell someone they look nice in what they are wearing, give a sincere compliment in a specific way on something they've done. Ask questions and get involved in a simple conversation. If the response is slight today, tomorrow may be better.

▶ Don't be afraid of your feelings. If you feel rejected, it won't kill you. After all, Walt Disney was once told his ideas about a cartoon with a mouse would have absolutely no appeal. He must have felt rejected too.

▶ Do something for somebody, get involved. Maybe for a long time now you've been thinking about volunteering as a

Candy Striper to read to little kids at the hospital. Or maybe you've read about teen-agers who did volunteer work on a teen-age crisis line called Dial HELP. Many said being involved helped them work through their own problems. Other kids you've read about did volunteer work with mentally retarded children. You've never had the courage before to think you could do something for someone else. But today's the day you start.

▶ Make the most of YOU. You have some interests, some talents, even though you may never have done much. Maybe you used to sing in the church choir and maybe you've always wanted to play tennis. So today begin to develop your inter-

ests. Join the school chorus. Sign up for the beginner tennis class after school.

Once your just-for-today campaign begins, you won't see the sky ablaze with rockets announcing the new you. But you are beginning. You'll have some setbacks, but doesn't everyone? Progress may seem like the fabled turtle in the race with the hare. But if you keep at it, you'll get where you want to be. There'll be lonely times, too. But they won't take you over and make you think you're always on the outside looking in. You will forget yourself in the finding of others.

As you become more involved in your world, you will nourish your self-esteem. A positive self-estimate is not conceited, feeling superior to others. It is the quiet comfort of knowing who you are. A good positive self-image will help you grow to be all that you can be.

CHAPTER FOUR

Parent Power

Children are not things to be molded,
But are people to be unfolded.

JESS LAIR

Have you ever heard someone say, "Adulthood comes about two years before parents admit to it and about two years later than teen-agers think"? Your relationship with your parents is changing from one of protection and dependence to, ideally, affectionate equality by the time you become an adult. This change often brings turmoil.

"What's wrong with parents," said Jana, "is that they knew

58

us when we were little. They perpetually remind us of our childhood. So they're the ones we need to shock. We've got to show them that we've changed."

On the parents' side, only yesterday you were their little child, needing and seeking their advice on the smallest matters. While parents seem to change very slowly (do they seem very different to you from the way they were two years ago?), you have changed almost overnight. It's hard for them to keep up with the new you, now caring a great deal about things that mattered not at all a short time ago. Two months ago you wouldn't be caught dead in anything but jeans and T-shirt. Now your mother can hardly believe her grubby football player wants a flower-print shirt and a white belt!

Then, too, there are times that you feel like saying, "Hey, no, I'm not ready. I don't want to be independent." You don't say it verbally, but your actions show it. You refuse responsibility for your belongings, as a child may do. You'd like to drive the car but don't want the problem of earning gas- or date-money. Yet you are charged with a whole battery of new emotions that say loud and clear, you're not a child anymore.

Why are communications between you and your parents so difficult? Mental-health and juvenile authorities say they constantly hear "Nobody listens." One psychologist says American homes are something like a railroad station, with everybody coming and going all the time. In the Pacific Northwest many communities recently proclaimed a Family Unity Month, and a brochure was published to show families how to spend "at-home evenings." This campaign may seem farfetched to some of you, but it speaks plainly and poignantly of the problems in our culture. Dad has a business meeting tonight, Tuesday night Mom has bridge club, your brothers have a Little League game Wednesday evening, you have class-play rehearsal Thursday, and Friday your parents have a dinner engagement. Saturday you have a date, and Sunday some family friends will visit, while all the children scatter in different directions. Does that sound familiar? Unfortunately for the family, such scheduling is all too common. Little wonder that no one has time to listen.

A Changing Relationship

Along with busy schedules, there are many other factors that bring parent power to the fore in your life just now. How your parents feel about you often produces conflict. Most—and possibly all—parents have mixed emotions about seeing their children become adults. Does that surprise you? For many years they nurtured you and worked to prepare you to be independent. As this goal comes within reach, their main job comes to an end. They then view the almost-finished product at sixteen or eighteen. Many parents feel they have not succeeded nearly as well as they had hoped. The impact of this realization creates a double problem. Parents think, "Well, maybe if I controlled more of his life, gave more direction, things would be better, success would be assured." The parent then tries to make more decisions for you, when you know the decisions should now be yours.

Your nearing adulthood may also provoke your parents to try to protect you from dangers they feel are much more serious than you realize. All the old fears and pains they knew, their unsolved problems well up in their memories. Mom remembers how difficult it was to stay within the sexual limits she had set for herself. Perhaps some guilt or shame is the fuel that ignites the parental explosion when Julie appears in a new string bikini that leaves nothing to the imagination. When Dad watches Scott go down to a ghastly defeat as he runs for student-body president, he recalls the pain he knew in a similar situation. He may then be clumsy when he speaks about it, or worse still, he may totally avoid talking to Scott about the defeat. To you, parents seem to be acting all wrong, uncaring or overreacting. They think they are simply sheltering you from harm.

There can be other factors too. For instance, a teen-age daughter can be threatening. Tanya's lovely, youthful figure and bouncy ways come at a difficult time for her mother, who feels very much in need of support herself. When she sees eager young men come calling, she feels the loss of her own youth. She may actually be jealous of Tanya, who can easily bring men's eyes to follow her.

Some women see themselves as less needed when their children are launched into the world. Both parents suddenly feel there's not much time left to influence their teen-agers, so they lay the advice on thick. My own children have been known to say, only half-jokingly, "Here comes Mother McGough's lecture Number Two."

A father may see his son as now having opportunities he was denied—for example, the chance to go off to college and prepare for a profession. He may also see you as a young man, full of ideals and ready to go out and conquer the world, and think wistfully of the goals he didn't quite reach. These thoughts can be damaging if your father can't handle them. Both parents may perceive you, the new generation, as the rising stars while they themselves are fading in power and influence.

Fathers and sons may have a sports rivalry also, as the son reaches peak athletic prowess. The son is strong, lean, and athletic, while the father may begin to lose his keen coordination, his hair may be thinning, and he may have developed a paunch. It's possible for a subtle resentment to be present, even if the father may not realize this or may be unwilling to admit it.

Some parents think of their children as insurance against loneliness in old age or as a financial source. As they see you form alliances with the opposite sex, they begin to feel replaced in your affections and to be afraid of losing you.

You may also be a considerable financial burden to your

parents. Middle-class families, particularly, feel the pinch of supporting teen-agers, who are busy dating, telephoning, cheer-leading, playing sports, using family cars, having beach parties, and bringing their friends home for snacks. Even unconsciously, hardworking families may resent these non-contributing consumers, even in cases where teen-agers earn some pocket money. Teen-agers cost more than adults to clothe and feed. Middle-class parents may also get squeezed when it comes to financing college educations, for scholarship aid is often not available for them, yet a college education is extremely expensive.

How to Communicate Better with Parents

▶ Remember that they need affection, too. Parents want to be loved and understood, just as you do. Take an interest in their life, in what they are doing, in their cares and their feelings. Try talking to one parent at a time when other siblings are not around. One family I know makes a habit of taking one teen-ager at a time along on an errand—sometimes a made-up errand—as a means of having a few moments alone with each other. Ask to go along with your father some evening when he heads for the hardware store or with your mother as she goes to the library. The quiet dark of a car is a good place to ask a parent how he or she feels about something important. On one such errand Lisa found the courage to ask her mother how she felt about abortions and if she thought girls under twenty-one should be able to have abortions without their parents' permission or knowledge. Sometimes parents are more uncomfortable talking about sex and morals than you are. The darkness will provide both of you with some shelter, a bit like the telephone crisis lines on which you can talk about your problems without having to face someone.

Alone with one parent, you can also share your feelings in such a way that they feel free to share theirs with you. You don't have to wear your heart on your sleeve or pour out all your sorrows—just show that you care about them enough to share some of your life.

▶ Let your parents know how strongly you feel. Introduce your subject by saying, "Mom, this is really important to me. Could we talk a little?" Or say, "I'm really worried about. . . ."

▶ Help your parents understand you. In Richland, Washington, under the sponsorship of the county Mental Health Center and Juvenile Court, teen-agers participated in town meetings for parents and young people. They called the program "Open Dialogue, 1975." Before the meetings took place teen-agers had many discussions to decide what they wanted to talk about. They felt that often parents didn't respect their individual rights, so they decided to define rights, privileges, and responsibilities. Below is a copy of the sheet they handed out on meeting nights. While you may not agree with all of their definitions, you can see that much thought went into preparing their discussions. All of the teen-agers on the panel agreed that where the most friction with parents occurred was over freedom of choice of friends, for both sexes and every age group.

OPEN DIALOGUE, 1975

RIGHTS

Definition: A right is something you are born with, are entitled to as a human being, and that should not be taken away.

1. The right to express your opinion and be heard and to have parents take the time to listen to you.
2. Freedom of choice about:
   (a) friends of both sexes and any age
   (b) clothes and appearance
   (c) career and to decide your own destiny
   (d) activities
3. Privacy of:
   (a) room and belongings
   (b) mail
   (c) phone
4. To spend your money the way you want.
5. To be consulted before plans or jobs are made for you.

PRIVILEGES

Definition: Something that is gained through responsibility.

1. To earn money through responsibilities.
2. To plan and attend activities that you choose and with whom you choose.
3. To be able to plan your own time:

(a) bedtime

(b) return time from activities

(c) TV time

RESPONSIBILITIES

Definition: a. Something you do as part of a group.

b. A means of developing yourself.

1. To make your own decisions whether right or wrong and learn from them.
2. Courtesy and respect for others, and other people should have as much courtesy and respect for you.
3. To try to do your best in everything you do.
4. To do what you feel you need to do to make life and living conditions a little easier, i.e., chores, etc.
5. To choose friends and activities that will contribute to your growth and development.

If you were a parent, would you allow your teen-ager to have complete freedom of choice to go out with friends of any sex and age? Debbie, seventeen, said she felt her parents had no right to tell her she could not go steady with her twenty-three-year-old boyfriend. She said she had nothing in common with boys her own age. Do you agree?

Another panelist, Dinah, fifteen, said her mother often listened in on her phone conversations. While most people would feel that privacy on the phone is important to everyone, you may also wonder why a parent would feel she needed to eavesdrop. Dinah was asked if her mother had reason to be suspicious. She answered, "Yes."

One boy, call him Mike, seventeen, said his only responsibility in his home was to take out the garbage once a week. As long as he did so, he could come and go as he pleased, could go out and come home two days later, no questions asked. He was asked, "Do you think that's all a home is for?" He said, "I guess not, but it works okay for me." He was also asked, "Do you feel loved, or that anyone cares about you?" He shrugged his shoulders.

In Daniel Offer's study of adolescent boys, 90 percent said they felt delinquency in high school was caused by parents who didn't care! The boys said the things they liked least about home were physical discomfort, sibling rivalry, and that home made them feel depressed. Other young people in a discussion group said they felt home should be a place where they could recharge their batteries, a pleasant place of refuge from the cold outside world, a place where they could share troubles and know that they were cared for.

What do you consider rights, privileges, and responsibilities of a teen-ager? When you ask for rights and privileges, can you accept the responsibilities, the consequences that go along with them? In many cases, parents are still legally responsible for your actions. Aside from their love or care for you, they have a legal stake in preventing you from doing wrong.

▶ Be aware of your parents' stresses. Like everyone else your parents have their own set of problems, insecurities, and tensions. Just as you usually cope with your problems on your own most of the time, so do they. But there are times when anxieties and problems get to be too much. Then their troubles will likely affect you too. Suppose your father has a new boss he doesn't like; he is considering a job change; the doctor has told him to lose weight. Can you see that he could be under stress and not as sympathetic to your plans and projects as you'd like him to be?

Your mother may seem impossible lately. You realize that your father has been traveling a lot. Your mother complains that she must do all the taxi service for your sister's piano les-

sons, your brother's baseball team. Your grandmother has recently moved in with you. Under these conditions, would you expect your mother to be more irritable than usual? No matter how important practicing to get your driver's license is to you, it may seem only a trifle to her.

► Are small things worth a big hassle? What may seem important today may actually be laughable in a few weeks. When you are in the midst of a major hassle with your parents, ask yourself, "Will this really matter six months from now?" If it won't, maybe it's not worth making a big issue of. For example, suppose the mess in your room absolutely infuriates your mother. While some mothers overdo the neat-and-clean bit, ten minutes of your time to make the bed and keep your room in order before you leave for school each day could go a long way to smooth relationships. An hour on Saturday to clean your room or to help with other housework can do wonders to lift the spirits of a busy mother, especially if she is working outside the home and still has to cope with family chores.

If your father hates rock music, is it such a big deal to keep your stereo turned down so he isn't blasted out of his chair while you enjoy your current favorite? In view of the energy shortage, is it essential to leave your radio playing all night just because you like to fall asleep to music? When your parents blow their cool over such things, it seems only sensible to change your ways, at least until you are no longer living under your parents' roof.

► Treat your parents as you'd like them to treat you. Respect your parents' activities, just as you expect them to respect yours. Don't poke fun at how silly and boring it would be to you to play bridge in the afternoon. Maybe your father enjoys science-fiction or horror movies, or maybe he's obsessed with sports on TV. That is his escape from the reality of the workaday world, and he's entitled to it. Lisa comments, "My mother's friends don't even know what's going on in the world, they are so wrapped up in their bridge playing and antique junk hunting. All my dad thinks of are the Saturday sports programs." While you may not understand their needs and desires for activities very different from yours, if you do not respect their tastes, how can you ask that they respect (if not understand) your need to play tennis at ten in the morning, horseback ride in the afternoon before you swim and sunbathe for two hours, and go to a dance at night?

A well-known New York fashion designer said her daughter turned away in disgust when she saw her mother dancing to a rock band. While you may feel some things are special to your life and you don't care to share them with parents, does this agree with your concept of "to each his own"? Just as you ask to be treated as an individual, parents should be allowed their own individuality. If you don't wish to be criticized, don't criticize them. If you don't like someone to snap at you, speak kindly to them.

▶ Put your parents' interests in front of your own sometimes. Everyone gets caught up in his or her own cares and interests many times. Most of us have been guilty of treating parents like furniture—just there, but not of any great use much of the time. Do you go along with your parents' plans? While no one expects you to get very excited about your father's boss coming to dinner, if you pitch in and set the table or sweep the front porch, your help will be appreciated. Family living is a cooperative affair. If you pitch in without being asked, or rearrange your busy schedule to suit family needs, home can be a happier place for everyone. How easy it is to have so many activities and interests that you constantly say, "I need . . . I want . . . Dad, can you. . . ."

▶ Keep communications open. Mark, fourteen, complains, "My parents never ask my opinion on anything important. They never let me in on any family problems. How can they pretend to understand me if they don't care enough to include me?" But Mark didn't mention that he was usually hostile to questions or attempts at conversation from his parents. Most of the time he holed up in his room, door tightly closed. His parents got the message, "This is my world, don't enter. Don't bother me."

If you come home from school and usually expect your mother to be there, don't you wonder where she is if she isn't there? If you find a note on the kitchen table, "Gone to the store, back by four," you are happy. The same works in reverse. Consider how your parents feel when they expect you to be home and you are gone with no explanation.

▶ Listen to the voice within. Some people seem hell-bent on a course of self-destruction. They feel miserable, they've done something stupid, and they hate themselves for it. Then they blame someone else, often their parents or someone they love. They lash out at them and hate themselves more. Nothing seems right in the world. They feel sad or mad that things haven't gone well. They won't make that same mistake again. They won't care about someone, so they won't get hurt. And on they go, hiding their real feelings from themselves, blaming unhappiness on the nearest person in sight. Listen to your feelings, define the issues.

You get into a big hassle with your mother over a mess you left in the kitchen, when this has nothing to do with your real anger. Look within. Very closely. Talk to yourself. You try to be mean to someone to make up for the hurt within that has nothing to do with him or her. Go back to where it all began. Get a dialogue going with yourself, and when the child in you has gotten you in trouble, make a decision to call a halt before it's too late. The first time you do this will be the toughest.

► Grab hold of your emotions. When you get into trouble with parents, the higher the level of emotions, the more difficult real communications are. When you see that emotions are running the discussion, back off. Both of you are likely to say things you don't mean and may later regret.

► Why can't we talk? Have you ever asked this question about your family? Of course, it's probably their fault. Right? Wrong! When families can't talk to each other, when any discussion breaks down into a heated argument, tears, recriminations, usually both parties bear some of the guilt. But blaming and guilt don't improve communications. Just as bad habits seem to be contagious, the little caring gestures can do wonders. Try showing your appreciation for small things done for you.

Find something positive to say to your parents. Unexpressed appreciation, lack of interest in each other, poor timing can develop into isolation. When you become emotionally isolated from your parents, you feel unsupported. They feel rejected.

At an airport restaurant in Hawaii on a steamy August day, I watched a harried mother handle a family situation. Her young son had just knocked a milk shake off the tray he carried. Her handbag slipped from her shoulder and spilled its contents on the floor. As she attempted to get her children settled at the table, a teen-age daughter asked if they could go to an airport

shop to look at a long dress. The mother said, "Please don't ask me now. It's just not a good time to talk about it." Instead of losing her temper, she gave the good reason for her lack of interest. Had she angrily said, "Good grief, *no!*" she would have cut off communication and put her daughter down for asking —a rejection.

The Diversion Project

A few years ago in Sacramento, California, juvenile authorities launched a Diversion Project to aid runaways, potential delinquents, to help keep them out of the juvenile court system. The means used was called family crisis intervention, a lofty-sounding term that helped open communications within families. The project handled about 100 cases a month. Most teenagers were between fifteen and seventeen years old. One part of the family-history questionnaire asked, "Have any of the following things happened to the family during the past year?" Families were asked to check as many as applied.

1. Death of a close family member? (Who?)
2. Divorce or separation
3. Birth of a child
4. Child or other relative moved out (temporary or permanent)
5. Child or other relative moved in (temporary or permanent)

6. Visit from some family member not ordinarily living in household
7. Serious household accident (serious enough to require a doctor)
8. Someone out of work one week or more
9. Someone lost a lot of money
10. Unpaid debts (payments past due)
11. Job change
12. Retirement of family member
13. Auto accident (serious)
14. Lawsuit
15. Family member in jail
16. Family member arrested [other than the child]
17. Driver's license revoked
18. Serious argument with someone within or outside the family
19. Excessive drinking (more than isolated episode)
20. None of the above

Both the parents and the runaway were given an extensive questionnaire to determine how each viewed their family life. Not surprisingly, in a high percentage of cases, teen-agers' actions reflected disruptions in the home, things going on that made them feel uncared about.

Lisa summed up the feelings of many troubled teen-agers: "Nobody listens. They think you don't know what's going on in your home. You get tied up in knots, and then you add to the troubles. After a while you can't take it anymore, so you run."

The Diversion Project workers feel that most young people are running *from* something—not running *to* something—and most would like to go home if things would change there. The teen-ager who acts out his feelings by running away is dramatizing a dysfunctional family, say juvenile authorities.

Frequently communications are called a two-way street. A leader in the Sacramento project defines communications as a three-way street: talking, listening, and understanding—from the speaker to the listener and back to the speaker. As they work with runaways and their families, they ask the listeners to rephrase what they've heard and repeat it back to make sure the receiver heard the right message. Try this with your family or with a friend.

On his side the teen-ager sees his action in terms of his need to grow, to develop self-identity, to find independence. The parent sees only rebellion, unsociable behavior, rejection. On the other hand, the child sees overcontrol, dominance, interference, lack of trust. Parents view themselves as concerned, wanting to do the best they can with what they can offer. Neither looks at the other point of view. Parents say, "There's nothing wrong with us. It's that mangy kid." And kids say, "They don't care." When a teen-ager runs away, he's hurting, and he needs help. The parents feel rejected, hurt, and angry. In the Diversion Project, parents and runaways were helped to face each other, to look at each other physically, to talk about their feelings—not just what someone did, but how they felt about their home life.

While you can't push a button and suddenly make everything

rosy, you can unlock the vise of blocked communication by getting your conflicts and worries out in the open.

Many families who have problems don't wind up with a young person running away to find help through a Diversion Project. But often seeking professional help is a wise route for a teen-ager to use. Here are some agencies you can find in the telephone book in your community, or you can ask a telephone operator to help you find the proper listing for your state or city: Catholic family service agency; Children's Society; Family Service agency; state, county, or city welfare department; state, county, or city mental-health department. Many cities also have telephone crisis lines or a crisis-intervention center.

While parents may seem now to have so much power over you, you also have tremendous power: that of giving love to them. If you think they haven't given you enough material things or enough love and guidance in meeting the world, consider that they may have given as much as they are able to. They give in proportion to their abilities, both financial and psychological.

Sometimes teen-agers build up such a wall of resentment toward parents that they are not willing to reach out to them. Dr. Haim Ginott told the story of a sixteen-year-old boy who tried on a suit. He said, "If my parents like this, is it okay if I return it?"

CHAPTER FIVE

You and the Rest of the World

And in the sweetness of friendship
let there be laughter, and sharing of pleasures.
For in the dew of little things
the heart finds its morning and is refreshed.
KAHLIL GIBRAN

How well do you get along with other people? What is the basis for liking and disliking someone? You constantly meet other people and size them up, while they in turn size you up. People manage to sort out others amazingly fast even when they are thrown together in the most novel situations.

79

For example, most members of the freshman class at a university have never met before. Yet in a few weeks many interwoven social relationships develop. Students classify each other, usually in categories based on how they see one another. When you move to a new town and start a new school, you may feel somewhat isolated for a while, adrift, apart from the whole. You meet a whirl of new faces. In a few weeks perhaps you have found a new friend, and the world is a brighter place.

How did you go about choosing this friend, or the friend in choosing you? First impressions, according to psychologists, are reasonably accurate, in spite of the minimal and inconsistent information people use to draw conclusions. Jana and Laurie moved to the same new neighborhood the summer before their sophomore year. They met at a local swimming pool. Jana saw Laurie come into the pool area and smiled a greeting as their eyes met. They soon discovered both were newcomers, both were wild about rock, pizza, and tennis in that order. The warmth of the first contact set the stage for friendship. Laurie was attractive, tall, and wore a zingy long beach robe. Had Laurie presented a sloppy, unappealing appearance, Jana might not have looked up.

Attraction and Friendship

When two strangers meet for the first time, they notice each other's way of dressing, the way they walk and talk, tone of voice, and other cues to make assumptions about each other. People may make inaccurate judgments from the sketchy information they get from the look in someone's eyes, his style of dress, the firmness of his handshake, etc. Yet they still classify by external things. Sometimes they stereotype others, placing them into a rigid slot based on a single characteristic, assuming they have a whole bundle of other associated behavior traits. A leather-jacketed, bearded motorcyclist hardly fits the stereotype of a rising young medical doctor.

Like Jana and Laurie, many choose their friends because they are similar, they like the same things, they are compatible with each other, they live near each other. Despite astrological

or other popular explanations, proximity, or physical nearness, is a major factor in deciding who will be friends; similarity of interests, how people meet each other's needs, and mutual admiration are also important.

If you live in California and your best friend is in Iowa, part of the pleasure of friendship is missing. You may write and spend a vacation together and still think absence makes the heart grow fonder. It also causes friendships to fade. People grow apart. You need to spend time with each other, to see and do things together, if friendship and close relationships are to continue. The boy on your street offers a more promising friendship than one a thousand miles away.

When you know someone shares your interests and attitudes, you have a more positive feeling toward them. You evaluate them with a plus if they agree with your values. Of course, opposites sometimes attract, with a friendship based more on how you complement each other than on your being carbon copies of each other. You need to talk; they need to listen. Your different needs are compatible. Quiet people, though, are generally more comfortable around others of reasonably quiet nature. Lynn and Alan got on well with each other. He was content to have her make decisions and mother him, while she enjoyed his easygoing, introverted nature.

Sometimes people have trouble with friendships because they habitually choose friends for the wrong reasons. Mike latched onto Brian because he was useful; he had his own car. Superstudents often find they have a lot of would-be friends hanging around, hoping to get help with homework. Ask yourself if Judy is your friend because you like to be with her or because you can push her around or because she has a neat wardrobe she'll share.

Girls are apt to want friends to be loyal, reliable, warm, and sensitive, ready with emotional support. Boys tend to want their friends to be with them in real trouble, as in fights or conflict with authority. Boys need a gang or group of pals who band together in a unified front.

Not every friend is your soul sister or brother, your closest confidant. Not every acquaintaince is a friend, although the term friend is often used loosely. You may have friends you go bowling with, friends you walk home from school with, and friends you do other things with. A close friend shares more than just the activities of life. She takes interest in things you do that don't include her, she admires and likes you. You accept her faults and virtues, just as she accepts yours. You trust each other. One day she is your acquaintance, and in a short time she is a close friend. Some friends are closer than others, and you need not expect or demand closeness from every same-sex friend you have. Some people need more friends than others. Some friendships happen quite naturally, while others have to be worked at more. All friendships wither and die if they aren't nourished. If you never see each other, never share things, it's hard to stay close. If you make plans to go to a movie and then break your date when something better turns up, your friendship may be headed for trouble. Friendships include responsibility. If your own interests always come first, you won't enjoy many friendships. Consider your friend's interest and welfare on an equal plane with yours. When a friend asks a favor and you hedge, they will be reluctant to go out of their way for you. Friendships imply loyalty and complete honesty. No one likes to be used so don't use your friend as a means to an end.

Suppose you invite Karla over for Saturday afternoon. You have no special plans. Some other girls call and ask you to join them to practice cheerleading, but they don't want Karla to come. They criticize her to you. Do you call Karla and beg off on your invitation? Or do you explain that she is a valued friend and while you want to come, you cannot? This group will respect you more for your loyalty, and they may learn to like Karla.

You will be a broader person if you have friends who are not mirrors of you. Of course, we don't usually choose a friend because he or she is completely different from us. However, a well-known psychologist said friendships as we grow up tend to be fleeting, each filling a need as we grow. For example, shy Sue and vivacious Vicky are good friends. Sue tries out or vicariously experiences another life-style as she sees Vicky storming along. While she knows she couldn't be such a flamboyant person as Vicky, it's fun to watch what she does closely and think about it. Chances are, Sue will move away from the friendship once her need is filled and she realizes this style isn't for her. Moving in and out of friendships as we grow is quite normal.

Being a friend means accepting someone as he or she is, not trying to make him or her over in your own image. Having a friend who has different interests and skills is interesting. If you have been strictly a bookworm, are you willing to join in the volleyball game your friend loves? Apart from your mutual interests, will you experiment with some of hers? While friendships come and go like the tides, sometimes stormily and sometimes gently, try to be flexible and not get yourself in a rut having friends only within your crowd, who are apt to be all much like you.

As with any relationship, friendships are not without problems. Jealousy and problems of communications both can dampen any friendship. If you find yourself teasing your friend, only half in fun, take a look inward. Do you resent that she was chosen cheerleader and you weren't? Are you envious of her artistic talents? A pang of jealousy is normal. But if you begin to gossip about your friend and snipe at her at every chance, persistent jealousy is taking over, and you should try to figure out why. Why not work harder to achieve for yourself what you envy her for? Or better yet, work on your own strengths so you needn't feel inferior.

When friendships falter, poor communications are sometimes the reason. When you are angry or disappointed, why not say so, calmly? Don't scold or be sarcastic. Tell your friend the way you feel, and the air will probably clear, or at least the discussion will pave the way for a sounder friendship.

Lisa commented, "She's nearby, and she used to be so comfortable to be with; now I feel like her punching bag. She's always putting me down." When a friendship isn't pleasant and makes you miserable, cut the ties, however painful doing so is.

Sometimes when a friendship has run its course, girls do

mean things to each other. They seem unable to part gracefully. Two boys described girls in their junior high: "One will take the other's perfume, spray it all over the ground, or throw junk on the other's locker shelf. This happens when two share a locker and have been good friends. Then they argue about it in the hallway where everyone can hear. After a heated argument, maybe even pushing one another, but rarely an all-out physical fight, each girl tries to get everyone on her side. They tell everybody what the other did, making themselves look completely innocent. Whatever caused the fight to begin with gets lost. They try to involve everyone."

Boys, however, resort to fistfighting when they want to establish their superiority. Often at the beginning of the school year, or just at the end, boys challenge someone to fight them. After the battle, the winner has lofty status.

Ninth-grader Mark drew this analogy: "When boys fight they're just like the baboons you see on TV or read about. They have to establish who's the top man. And once they do, everybody knows it."

"Is it really possible to have a close friend of the opposite sex and not be romantically involved?" This question was discussed in several junior-high-school classes. While many students said that such a relationship was possible and that they had at some time tried it, most felt that one of the pair usually developed a crush on the other, causing the friendship to split. A number of ninth-grade boys thought that of course they could have a girl for a special friend, particularly on an intellectual level. What do you think?

New friends can be stimulating and don't always mean that old ones get shunted to one side. You can have both if you choose. Once you have a new close friend, don't quickly pour out all the confidences a former friend has shared. Nothing is less gracious than a gossip. Also, your new friends will wonder what you'll say about them. As one high-school student wrote, "If you were another person, would you like to be a friend of yours?"

Dating, Rating, and Mating

What do you think about dating? Do you see dating as a means to an end or an end in itself, a fun-and-games popularity contest? Perhaps you have never thought about dating as a passport to somewhere, a ticket to finding the right mate in life or deciding whether you wish to marry. However, many psychologists feel this is the true function of dating.

While certainly it's fun to have a partner for school functions, that partner may rate high as a date, low as a mate. In surveys asking what characteristics are valued for a date and for a marriage partner, some not-surprising differences appeared. People listed in order such desirable qualities for a date as: physically attractive, nice personality, considerate. For a marriage prospect, however, the qualities rated in this order: considerate, similar values and attitudes, intelligent, physically attractive, responsible. Men consistently rate physical attractiveness higher than women do in choosing a mate. In a computer-dating study, researchers R. H. Combs and W. F. Kenkel reported that college males placed more emphasis on the physical than females did. It seems acceptable in our culture for men to select women for sex or physical appeal, but not for women to select men this way. Women supposedly prize security and warmth above superficial attractiveness.

There is an important link between dating and mating. Through dating you learn to communicate with members of the opposite sex. You learn to evaluate and to be comfortable with them. You learn to know different people before you finally settle on a permanent mate. Here are some guidelines to bear in mind in your date life.

▶ Don't be onstage. Let your date see the real you. When you date, it's easy enough to be on your best behavior, acting at being something you're not. You find that he or she loves classical music, so you profess an appreciation of it, although you hate it. It is much easier to say, "I don't really appreciate it, but I'll listen to be with you." Don't adopt all his or her attitudes and suddenly find you've lost your own personality. If you are pliable and agreeable to anything, and this relationship should someday lead to marriage, will you want to continue that role?

▶ Crowd dating is fun, but what's your date like alone? The trend is more toward crowd dating now than to isolated twosomes. And being with others does help with conversation and let you get to know your date's group behavior. Still, vary the double dates with times spent alone. One counselor said he

had stopped being surprised to learn that many engaged couples had never been out alone! Even if your relationship is not serious, you should be on your own some of the time. You'll learn things about each other that you would not see in a crowd. And, when all is said and done, marriage is not a group affair.

▶ Is going steady worth the price? Cindy, seventeen, and Steve have been a steady twosome since they were sophomores. Says Cindy, "It's really boring sometimes. We have nothing new to say to each other. He just comes over every night all summer. We watch TV. My folks think he's a fixture." Of course, they had an automatic date for every school function and for any school picnic. Oddly enough, they knew the relationship was dull, but neither had the courage to break off. They were too insecure to let go of each other. At a time in life when both should have been learning to get along with different personalities, they were stagnating and not growing. If you do go steady, however, don't be afraid to admit it if your feelings change. Far better to lose a steady date than to get locked into an unhappy situation permanently or suffer a broken marriage.

▶ He/She promised to change! Advice columnists hear this comment all the time about troubled marriages. Forget it. It's not likely that you can reform someone or make him or her over to your ideal. If you cannot accept your friend as he or she is, find someone else to share a lifetime with.

▶ Check out communications. Can you talk to your special date? If you seriously consider this person as a future mate, evaluate your ability to communicate with each other. Advice columns are filled with letters from people who complain, "We can't talk to each other. We have nothing to say to each other anymore." If you can't share your deepest thoughts, your fears and hurts, your goals and ideals, if you never go beyond superficial small talk, how much can you really know about him? Or her?

▶ Go slowly. Don't find yourself trapped in a dating game that's all physical. While most dating has some physical expression of pleasure, a relationship that starts with necking and petting may get out of hand in a hurry. Physical attraction and love are quite different and need not go together.

▶ Love and sex are easily confused. Both boys and girls need to recognize and understand that there are great biological differences between them. Sexual desire in boys comes in a rush of emotion and an immediate, specific desire, separate from feelings of love. A boy's sexual feelings are usually very strong and can be easily aroused, but boys are also more casual about sex. Most girls are not able to separate romantic love from physical attraction and are apt to think being in love is necessary in order to have sexual relations. Consequently, girls read deeper meaning into an encounter than boys do. Obviously, the consequences will affect the girl more, so she can always refuse. A boy is not physically hurt when aroused and not gratified, even though he may be angry. He may even be relieved that she is not an easy mark, although this kind of double standard is now on the wane.

Some psychologists say that premarital sex can harm later sexual compatibility, particularly if there is much fear and guilt. Despite the freedom with which sex is treated in our society, many girls, and boys as well, first learn to view sex as a sinful, guilty pleasure. Aside from the physical dangers of venereal disease or pregnancy, the psychological toll can be great. Sexual compatibility doesn't happen overnight, and guilt doesn't help. Also, when sex is easily available, it may become the primary function of the relationship, at the expense of developing deeper ties. For girls especially, because they tend to invest more emotion in sexual intimacy than boys, this can lead to painful disappointment when the relationship fails to develop.

▶ You can choose which route you'll travel. At a teen seminar during a discussion of sex, a psychiatric social worker illustrated the possible choices. "The choices are like branches on a tree," he explained, as he sketched a branching tree. "If you choose to have sex freely, you have one set of situations to cope with. Choose the other route, and you have a whole different set. If you think it's worth the risk, you must decide this for yourself. Unfortunately," he went on to explain, "many teen-agers don't make conscious decisions. They are existential. They live only for this moment. They come to us and say, 'I didn't plan on this. It just happened.'" Too often having intercourse does "just happen" in adolescence. A research study on pregnancy in early adolescence found that most pregnant girls had not believed it could happen to them! This counselor told of the times in his community when the number of teen pregnancies skyrocketed. "When kids go to the state basketball championships, and when the hydroplane races are in town, look out. There's plenty of beer and partying. They say, 'We were all at this hotel, and no one quite knows how it happened.'" If you choose not to have sex freely, avoid situations that set the stage for sex.

▶ If you've made a mistake, don't wallow in self-pity. Mistakes should help us grow, not drag us down. Don't marry to preserve your honor or someone else's, unless you are in love and want to spend your life with this person. A girl may feel secondhand and that her chances for finding another mate are not good. A boy certainly has responsibilities he must face if his girl friend becomes pregnant. Neither of them, however, should feel pressured into marriage. Immaturity can easily blind you to personality traits that you know would make a miserable marriage. Should you walk away from this involvement? Of course, rather than begin a marriage on a shaky foundation.

▶ Don't use sex because you need contact comfort. Some girls have an intense need to be touched, to be held, and they give in to pressure for sexual intercourse to be cuddled. They feel alone and need warmth. All people have tactile needs. In times of stress, the need to be touched increases. One girl who appeared in juvenile hall explained, "I wanted to say 'hold me, just hug me,' and boys always think you want to have sex." There is no reason why a girl cannot make this distinction clear to a boy. Boys should realize that because a girl wants to be hugged and caressed may not mean she wants to have intercourse. Even if she does, however, a boy should not feel he must respond whether he wants to or not.

Statistically, teen-age marriages are poor ones. A study of 1425 high-school marriages showed that 20 percent of them ended in divorce within three years—three times the number of divorces for the first three years of marriage in the general population. Why do so many young marriages fail? Psychologists tell us that in the teen years most people are deeply involved in the "identity crisis." They are only beginning to grapple with a life stage called intimacy. Eric Erikson calls intimacy "the ability and interest in relating closely in both the physical and psychological senses." The desire to care for others is a stage well beyond the teens, researchers say. Thus, the average adolescent has much personality growth ahead before he is mature enough for parenthood. To nurture a totally dependent life, a child, and fit your existence into his, to give without receiving appreciation and understanding, demands infinitely more than most can give while they are still teen-agers.

About one half of all high-school brides are pregnant. Most drop out of school when their pregnancy is known or at least to have their baby. They rarely return to school. Limited in education, they have to settle for vocational goals far short of their dreams. Many later feel "cheated, that life has passed me by." Young husbands resent the economic burden of a wife and child at a time when they wish to continue their education or get started in a vocation.

The insecurity of modern life may push young people to seek the loyalty, affection, and warmth they think they'll find in marriage. The media show a glamorous picture of young marrieds. Friends are getting married young. Parents may offer financial help for the early years. Yet economics aside, the average teen-age marriage begins with two strikes against it—the maturity level of two people.

Use of Authority, When You Have It

Have you ever been elected as a class or club officer? If you are asked to be a leader, does the prospect scare you to death? When you do have authority, how do you use it? Does holding that office go to your head, make you feel you can order anyone to do your bidding? How do your classmates feel about your power?

A leader in any group decides what gets discussed, what and how jobs are accomplished. An effective leader is usually an outgoing person and one who can make decisions and organize things. He should make himself heard, but more important he must also open communications within the group for all ideas to be heard. Are you a catalyst to bring out the best in others? Can you delegate jobs, or do you feel, "to get it done right, I have to do it myself."

Marta, class president, felt harried and hassled, as she tried to get the student carnival organized. She went around the community seeking prizes, went to the printer to get tickets printed, made posters, worked on a booth, etc. To Marta, authority meant if no one volunteered, she had to do the job. Had she guided discussions more effectively to involve others, she might have found ideas other than her own. But she had forced her ideas on the group and so left herself wide open for a mountain of work. A mature leader accepts the responsibility that goes with authority but recognizes that real effectiveness is within the *entire* group. Marta needed to learn to work with others and not feel threatened if she shared authority with committees. Classmates have knowledge, skills, and ideas too. The majority vote might not have been for Marta's plan, yet she should not have felt undermined to accept someone else's plan. She was unable to give others credit and support their ideas. When things went wrong, Marta lost her temper. She did not know how to compromise or admit mistakes.

If you are chosen to be a chairman or leader, think about the purpose for which your group exists. This will help you do some advance planning before you preside over a meeting. Before you call a meeting to order, list on a blackboard the things to be accomplished that day. In the meeting ask the

group for suggestions, alternatives your group can choose from. As each person makes suggestions, he will be offering things he is capable of supporting. The key to leadership is effective communication. A good leader is one who sees that communication occurs.

Body Language

Every message you send has more to it than merely the words you speak. In fact, psychologists say that communications have three parts: verbal, or choice of words (7 percent of the message); vocal, the sound of voice (38 percent); and body language, or movements and posture (55 percent).

If more than half your message comes from body language, or nonverbal communication, perhaps you should take a closer look at the messages you send and at the ones you receive. What message do you send? Friendly, cool, hostile? Receptive, closed, defiant?

From eye contact to body postures, you have a whole silent language. But it's not a hidden language. For people all send and receive these messages to one extent or another, often in their subconscious. They get the message, but they're not sure how it came to them. You know that some people dislike you, yet they may have never said an unkind word directly to you. Perhaps they merely avoid making eye contact with you. Or they unconsciously turn their body away from you in conversation.

You can't take an isolated gesture, and say, "This body language means this." The whole context of the situation, what is being said, or not said, who is present, how close you stand, and so forth, must be considered. Nonetheless, here are a few brief tips that might clue you in to what's happening. Eye contacts are an important facet of body language. Eyes can challenge or defy, show love or hate, anger and despair. The person who can't look you in the eye is not someone you trust. They may just be shy or they may be sneaky. In either case, the effect is the same. You feel cool toward them. When you give a speech or talk to a group of friends, the amount of eye contact you make influences how well they receive your words. You also get feedback. Are they with you? Or out in left field dreaming? Is their posture attentive—leaning forward, neck outstretched, toward the front of the chairs—or are their arms tightly folded across the chest, as if to block communication? In close conversation, eyebrows have a variety of signals. They shoot up sometimes as if to say, "Are you sure of that?" Or, "Repeat the message, it's not clear to me." Tune in, don't keep blindly stumbling along when you see these messages. Say, "I see that you aren't with me. What did I say that troubles you?" You may be surprised to see how communication improves when you are aware of the total message.

Think of the body language a shy girl shows when she walks into a room. She makes no eye contact with anyone, doesn't smile or nod hello. Her body language says she is aloof and afraid of making contact. So in return she gets no positive feedback from the group. No warmth generated, none returned. Now think of swinging Suzy when she enters the group. She displays a whole different set of gestures, smiles, eye contact, and nods.

Watch for body messages from everyone around you. When you want to ask your father a favor, check out his nonverbal message. Does he walk flat-footed and shoulders slumped, as if to say that the world's undone him today? Or does he have a springy, bouncy walk that shows, "It's been a good day." Does he appear intense, worried, absorbed in some problems he couldn't leave behind? Take stock of when he is receptive to your needs.

In a discussion with someone, how good are you at controlling your emotions? Inner feelings often slip out in impatiently tapping fingers, a dangling, swinging foot, that says, 'Hey, let's get on with it." You may unconsciously turn your shoulders away in an anxious effort, or you make furtive glances toward the nearest exit. If you are threatened by what the other person has to say, then you may tune out. You may not be totally aware that you have tuned out, but your nonverbal behavior says, "Bug off." If the message you have to deliver is threatening to the receiver, or listener, then he resists your communications. Have you ever made the old eye-rolling gesture, eyes rolled upward when a teacher is talking to you? Maybe you accompany your nonverbal message with a barely audible *Tsk*. In either case, this says, "Okay, I've heard it all before." How do you think people feel when you do this? It antagonizes them, of course. No doubt you get a few negative messages from them in return,

including angry eyes, knit brows, pointing fingers, or clenched fists.

Personality types, too, can be discovered by body language. The introvert makes little eye contact and has a much harder time getting involved with others. The extrovert looks you in the eye often, lets you know he cares about you, a warm feeling. Do you know someone you feel good to be around? Does he or she make much eye contact with you? An introvert needs a big space bubble around him. If you stand too close, you invade his bubble, make him uncomfortable. An extrovert doesn't need quite so much body space, or territory, around him. You can also demonstrate a sense of personal territory by simply taking your brother's regular seat at the breakfast table. Or sit in someone's usual seat in a classroom or lunchroom. Chances are you'll get at least a dirty look, if not something louder from each person whose territory you invade.

The sense of touch, or tactile need, is also a broad facet of body language. Touch can be comforting or it can repel you. A tender pat on the hand may say, "There, there, everything will be all right." Or the unwanted touch of someone leaning against you in a crowded elevator can be awful. Some of us like to touch, to hug, shake hands, make physical contact, while others of us would rather not. Start watching body language, your own and other people's. It's interesting as well as helpful.

CHAPTER SIX

Why Do Anything?

When we do nothing,
we run the risk of becoming nothing.
PAUL GOODMAN

Do you ever wonder why some people get so much more accomplished than others? What drives the person who manages to do well and happily the many things you have only wished you could get around to?

Psychologist Carl Rogers defines motivation as something that propels action, originating from within the person who acts. For example, you eat because you are hungry. You drink because you are thirsty. You sleep because you are tired. These three are basic psychological motives, or drives, necessary to stay alive. Most people in developed countries take satisfaction of these basic needs for granted without thinking much about them. You are more concerned about self-motivation in less basic forms. While everyone seems to need activity, some people take flight, while others plod along, day after day, wondering if this is all there is to life.

Motivation

Why are some motivated and others not motivated? Why do you do something, and why do you not do something? Why did you go to school today? Why do you read a book, or why don't you? Why does a man like Evel Knievel do daredevil stunts on a motorcycle?

Once our basic needs are satisfied, how do we progress to greater things? Social researchers don't agree on what it is that motivates people, on which need produces what behavior. But they do agree on several things:

▶ All of us have needs. They are physical, psychological, or social.

▶ Anything we do has a goal.

▶ All actions are intended to achieve a goal.

▶ If we reach our goal, this will satisfy a specific need or want.

A man who never has enough food to eat will not likely walk in the forest and write a beautiful sonnet about his experience. Until our basic needs are met, we cannot move on to less essential things.

Psychologist Abraham H. Maslow studied human behavior and formed this important theory: People who are mentally and physically healthy need to achieve just as much as they need to eat and sleep. He says that you are born with a need to do something well. Maslow concluded that man is a constantly wanting animal and "that his needs are never fully met. As one need is met, another arises." When that need is fulfilled, again another arises. He places our motives, or needs, in a ranking order, from the lowest to the highest, in a pyramid form. His pyramid is constructed as follows:

FIRST LEVEL, PHYSICAL NEEDS

If you are always hungry, have never been satisfied, you consider the need for food your only need. About one fourth of the people on earth spend their whole life in search of food, shelter, and basic needs.

SECOND LEVEL, SAFETY NEEDS

You must be free from pain and fear. Maslow says that the need for order is part of this level and that through regular routine you make some order and sense of the world to help fulfill this need. When you are unfairly treated, you feel unsafe, insecure. All people react with fear when their safety is threatened.

THIRD LEVEL, LOVE NEEDS

When you reach this level, you already have food and shelter, but you feel the need to be with others, to be part of a group, to be cared for, and to care for others. He says that people in underdeveloped parts of the world do not have to deal with problems of getting or giving love. They have troubles on a lower level, while people in developed countries may have problems in giving themselves to others.

FOURTH LEVEL, ESTEEM NEEDS

Maslow says that you have the need to feel good about yourself, to have self-respect, and secondly, to have others think well of you. Once you learn what society values, you set out to get it so others will give you recognition. Many people think making a lot of money is a valuable trait, and some people satisfy their esteem needs by setting out to make a lot of money. Esteem needs continue throughout your life, however. You need to feel valued as a person, not just because you can make a lot of money.

FIFTH LEVEL, NEED FOR SELF-ACTUALIZATION

This, the topmost level on Maslow's pyramid, is not reached by everyone. For not all are able to achieve self-fulfillment. The need exists in all people, however, even if they are not aware of it. Maslow defines this need as, "The need to become everything that one is capable of becoming." In one person this drive may be expressed in being a fine biologist, in another, in being a wonderful parent. Maslow feels that understanding, including the need for knowledge, plays an important part in this level. Meaningful work, the need to excel at it, to do the very best that one can, is what gives meaning to people's lives. This accomplishment satisfies.

Maslow and other scientists who work with his theories believe that everything people do can be explained by the needs on the pyramid. They are either trying to meet and satisfy those needs, or they are reacting to their attempts to meet them. For instance, you may react with the anger of frustration when you can't reach a goal.

Take a look at the activities of your own day. Can you explain them in view of Maslow's theories? Of course, you'll probably find many mixed motives, not one clear-cut explanation for an action. Can you see someone else's behavior in terms of Maslow's ideas?

Here are some suggestions that may help you scale the mountain of motivation and help you to accomplish your goals:

▶ Stop kicking yourself all the time. Regrets, recriminations, and guilt are tough burdens to bear. Once you've made a mistake, don't bring it up all the time, effectively kicking yourself over and over again. Some people insist upon telling others how stupid they themselves are, what a dumb thing they did. If you feel you must make an apology for something, do so simply and quickly. Often no one will notice your goof or would think very little of it. If you make a big deal of it, you only convince others that yes, you are a dummy and reinforce your low opinion of yourself. And you make it harder for yourself to pay attention to achieving whatever goal you are after.

▶ Don't feel guilty if you succeed. While on the surface this may seem to be a strange statement, it's actually the case for many people. For instance, some psychologists say that many women avoid success. While at the University of Michigan, Matina Horner studied responses and feelings about success. She used stories her subjects were asked to complete. One story began: "After first-term finals, Anne finds herself at the top of her medical-school class." Men got the same story, with the name John substituted. Try completing the story yourself in three sentences.

Horner found that many women feared that success in competitive achievement would bring negative consequences—unpopularity or loss of femininity. Only about 10 percent of males responded with doubts and fears about success. Some women completed the story by saying, "Anne felt guilty. She will finally have a breakdown, quit med school, and marry a successful doctor." Others described Anne as lonely, acne-faced, socially rejected. Still other women turned the story around to describe Anne as a nurse or second in her class, not first. Horner feels that this anxiety stems from the way women have been brought up in our culture, to think that women who achieve outside the home are unfeminine or hard. Until these feelings of guilt can be resolved, women will not likely make the most of their opportunities. Nor will any man who is afraid to succeed, for whatever reason.

▶ Trust yourself. Don't be afraid to question authority.

Blind obedience to some authority figure can lead you to miserable situations, even to crime, and at the very least it deprives you of your self-esteem, your feeling of being a person in your own right, able to determine your own behavior.

For example, Stanley Milgram made a study of obedience. He wanted to see how many people would obey orders when they were told to do things that were clearly wrong. He told his subjects that he was conducting a learning experiment to study the effect of punishment on memory, to see if pain—and how much pain—helps people learn.

Lots were drawn to see who would be "teachers" and who would be "learners." The learners were strapped into an electric chair, while the teachers sat by generators and switches. On order from the experimenter, the teacher threw the switch to give shocks when learners made a mistake in memorizing pairs of words. When the teacher threw the switch, a red light came on, blue lights flashed, buzzing generators sounded, and a machine clicked. On wrong answers the teacher was told to increase shocks. The experimenter told teachers that shocks would be painful, but not dangerous. The instrument panel contradicted him, showing shocks as Slight, Moderate, Severe, or XXX. As shocks went over 300 volts, learners pounded on the wall. More shocks were given, and more wall pounding came—then deadly silence!

The teachers, however, did not know that the experiment was rigged. All slips said "teacher," and the learner was a stooge, who actually got no shocks at all.

A disturbing 65 percent of the teachers kept shocking to the highest voltage; 13 percent refused to go on after the first protest from the learner; 22 percent stopped before they got to the worst levels. Teachers showed they knew their action was wrong. They sweated, wrung their hands, looked worried. But they continued to inflict pain, as the authority told them to. Since this experiment was done at a reputable university, Yale, subjects were more easily induced to believe it was "in the interest of science." Away from the university setting, only 48 percent obeyed orders to continue shocking. You can very likely think of other times blind obedience to a leader or authority has made people do miserable things, or even commit crimes, whether on a national scale or much closer to home.

School Problems

In a study of adolescent personal problems using a 4000-student sample, researchers found that at least one half the school population was anxious about schoolwork. Boys worried more about academic studies than girls did, and they felt that while academic work was their own biggest problem, it was also their peers' biggest problem. One boy called school "a giant pressure cooker." Both sexes suggested that solving the problem through their own efforts was more important than finding an outside source for help. For example, more said they should "spend more time on homework" than those who felt they should "get my parents to help with my homework."

One researcher has observed that grades seem to nosedive

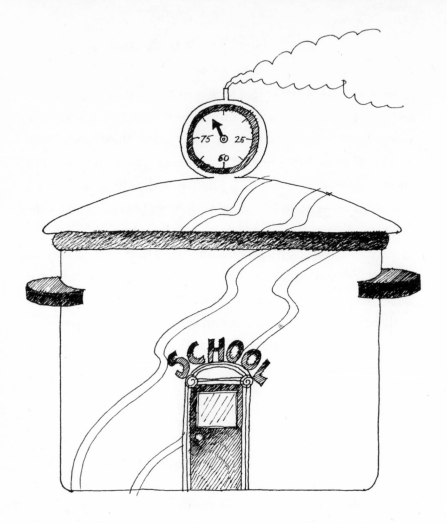

around ninth and tenth grade. He suggested that this dive may be caused by the beginning of regular dating and the increased awareness of the opposite sex. Interpersonal relationships begin to take much time and energy.

In many schools, the subcultures actually act as a negative influence on academic performance. The kids seen as "intellectuals" are not always those with the highest intelligence. They may be the only ones who are willing to work at a relatively unrewarding activity—unrewarding for this stage of life. As one student said, "It's hard to keep priorities sorted out. I really know where I should be putting my energies, and the pressure to do well to get into college is definitely there. But you gotta be part of the crowd too." No one would argue that finding that balance is a tough job. In groups you find more immediate rewards such as activity, interest, and involvement. In one study students were asked, "What would you rather do, flunk an exam or eat alone in the cafeteria?" How would you answer? Students in the study responded overwhelmingly that they would rather flunk an exam.

Perhaps just knowing that you are pulled in two different directions and sorting out your feelings about the problem may help you push and pull in the direction most important to you in the long run—not always the direction that brings immediate rewards and glories of the moment. Poor school performance may stem from any of several causes:

▶ Major distractions such as opposite sex, sports, etc.

▶ Sudden physical growth, which demands adequate nutrition and plenty of rest. One mother of teen-agers complained loudly about the size of her grocery bill. She was shocked to learn that the caloric needs of a teen-age boy are 3000 to 3500 per day! It helped to know that he really needed all that food.

▶ Rapid sexual development.

▶ Readjustment of relationships with peers and adults. The surge toward independence and the fight to make your own decisions can interrupt the concentration on schoolwork. But now more than at any time of life you set your own standards, discover what is of value to you.

The tasks of adolescence are not minor, but in the words of psychologist Erik Erikson, "without conflict, development does not occur." So, the crisis that you face does not imply chaos in your life but is typical of problems you see in any major transitional period. All routes through adolescence are not the same either. One person finds the path to maturity full of snags and snarls. Another finds it only mildly bothersome.

Homework and Test Taking

Test taking can be one of the biggest hassles of the school years. Why take tests in the first place? One answer is to think of tests as a way to diagnose your educational illness. Once you have the diagnosis, you can seek proper treatment. Tests show your strong points as well. A teacher gives a test to measure how much or how well students have learned the material presented in the course. They can then see what material was successful, and what needs to be worked on more. Tests help the teacher measure all students by the same yardstick.

Schools haven't cornered the market on tests, for more tests of one kind or another face you all your life. In whatever career you pursue, someone will be testing your knowledge, evaluating how well you know your stuff. If you are a salesman, an engineer, a plumber, or a schoolteacher, your customers or your supervisors will check your ability to do the job. Whatever you do will be measured and appraised. A good way to learn to handle future tests is to cope with the formal tests and exams you have in the classroom today.

Psychologists say the best time to begin studying for an exam is the first day of the course! Start in at the beginning of the course, keep a separate notebook or section of your notebook for each course, and have a systematic plan of attack. Look over class notes each day, see if the concepts presented begin to link together in your mind. Long-range preparation includes study and review of about one hour each week. If you ignore this practice, you face a test with two strikes against you. Ideas stick better if they are allowed to develop gradually during the term. Before-exam preparation could include a one-hour study session in which you change your manner of study once or twice during the session. Think of possible questions your teacher might ask. Review the areas of study, to be sure you understand all material fully. Ask the teacher if the exam will be essay, true-false, or multiple choice. Often a test is a combination of all three. Review with a friend, asking each other questions you think might be covered.

▶ What to study. The vocabulary of any course is usually an important part of any test. Do you have any printed handouts the teacher has given as study aids? What material was covered in the course in addition to the text? Go through your notes and underscore new words. Do you know their meaning and how they are related to each other, what role they play in concepts presented? In math and science courses rules, formulas, and laws should be reviewed. Relationships between things and events should be studied. To answer a question like "show the development of the major events that led to the Revolutionary War," you not only need to have a storehouse of facts, you need to see their relationships to each other.

▶ Don't forget your body. Many students work hard to prepare their mind for exam week, but they forget their body. A bone-tired body won't allow its mind to do fresh thinking. Cramming all night is like placing one foot in quicksand. The harder you struggle to learn months of material, the more quickly you become confused and frantic. You become so worried and fearful, you get to the classroom in a disorganized state. You forget even the few things you thought you knew. Get a good, normal night's sleep, eat a nutritious breakfast, and dress comfortably for the test.

▶ How to improve retention. Many scientists have studied the learning processes. One group of researchers studied the effects of sleep on memory. They found that subjects who studied pairs of words just before a deep sleep, called stage four sleep, appeared to remember what they learned. Some subjects learned the words and then went on with a normal waking activity before they were tested for retention. Other subjects did the learning tasks and were allowed to sleep only during early sleep stages, called REM (rapid eye movement) sleep. This pattern seemed to interfere with the learning process. The scientists urged caution in interpreting their experiments, but the results seem to make sense. Try learning something before you go to bed at night, when you have little interference from the time of learning until you try to recall that material in the morning. It may work for you, although there are many variable factors involved in any such attempt to improve retention of learned material.

For most kinds of material, spaced learning is more efficient than one block of time. Four fifteen-minute periods usually proved to be more effective than one solid hour of practice in some learning experiments, depending on the material to be learned.

What you do between the time of learning and the time of recall appears to be important, as substantiated by many researchers. People could recall six out of ten nonsense syllables they had learned just before sleep, where only one could be recalled by subjects who stayed awake after learning.

Whole learning is more efficient than learning in parts and then trying to piece it all together like a jigsaw puzzle. Material can be learned in parts if they logically relate to each other. For example, the following groups of words: 1. North, man, red, spring, woman, easy, autumn, yellow, summer, boy, blue, west, winter, girl, green, south. 2. North, south, east, west, spring, summer, autumn, winter, red, yellow, blue, green, man, woman, boy, girl.

You can learn better when you understand the meaning. It is easier to remember if you grasp the overall meaning and can relate material or associate it with what you already know. The way you organize learned material in your mind is vital to storage in your memory bank and later retrieval.

That all-important force, motivation, contributes much to how you learn. If you know you need this material and will put it to use in your life, you learn it quicker than if you have little interest in it. You may need it only long enough to take a test, but that's a motivation, too. You learn a foreign language in a country much more quickly if you need the language to get along. If most people in the country speak your language also, you may have little need of the new language.

Sometimes you can't remember something because you really never learned it in the first place. For example, you look up a phone number, dial it, then have to look it up again a few moments later. You never transferred the number to your long-term memory. With constant repetition of the same number, you then learn it. You automatically go to the right drawer when you want a fork to eat with, for you have learned by constant repetition where it's kept.

The Test Itself

Have your past tests indicated that you came to them poorly prepared? If so, work differently this time, and from now on. A modest success breeds more success. Anxiety over exams can paralyze you, and superhigh anxiety actually interferes with doing any complex activity. On test day, find a way to

keep your cool. Do whatever relaxes you, from prayer, meditation, to yoga and taking a deep breath. Wiggle your fingers, or wear your lucky charm.

Wearing the lucky bracelet, sweater, red hat, or whatever, is a kind of reinforcement, like a bribe to yourself. Every time a famous golfer wore a certain shirt, he won the tournament. The shirt became his trademark. People become superstitious about their lucky charms.

▶ Recognize that you are not mentally ill or unstable if you get a bit tense when you take a test. Keep your perspective.

Some stress actually gets your adrenalin going and pushes you to do well, as when a swimmer stands on the diving block before a meet.

► Arrive in the classroom with all the materials you need. If you are allowed a slide rule, computer, dictionary, or whatever, be sure to have it ready.

► Budget your time. How long is the test? Look it over quickly. If there are some sections that represent more points than others, leave yourself enough time to do them carefully. If you get stuck, move on, putting a check mark on that one to go back to after you've finished the ones you do know.

► Read all directions carefully. Some sections may have different instructions.

► Look for leads in one question that will help you answer others.

► Proofread all your answers before you hand in the test.

► A test doesn't evaluate you as a person. It's only a score on how well you understand the material. One test isn't your entire school career or your life.

CHAPTER SEVEN

Values

What you are speaks so loudly
I cannot hear what you say.

VOLTAIRE

In Arthur Miller's *Death of a Salesman*, Willy says, "I can't take hold, Ma. I can't take hold of some kind of life." Like a tiny boat adrift in a stormy sea, Willy couldn't seem to find any meaning in life. He was chronically unhappy, a misfit. We all know people who stumble through life like Willy, feeling worthless.

At a recent meeting of educators in the United States, the

participants talked about a different emphasis in our schools. Many felt that education should actually be a "search for values." Whose values, and which ones, shall schools teach? Can values *be* taught? How do you "get" values, and what are they anyway? We measure ourselves by the things we value. Values are something you hold onto, principles at the nucleus of your life. Values have been called "those elements that show how a person has decided to use his life."

A discussion of values can be like unfolding a road map. It can give you some idea of where you are going, although there may be a few detours along the way. It should help you raise questions, see alternatives, and consider all the possibilities for making important decisions in your life. Is it bad not to have a value-system? If you have no means of value-related decision making, then you probably miss out on full use of your potential.

All the things you do are based on your beliefs, attitudes, and values, either conscious or unconscious. How do you develop beliefs and values? Traditionally adults have moralized, brainwashed, and browbeat children, hoping that offspring will do what parents think is right. Or they give a model to follow, set a good example. Some parents who think that everybody has to find his own way just shrug and hope that things will turn out all right. You don't need or want adults to run your life for you. Yet some guidance helps sort out the confusion and conflicting advice you get from all sides. You see examples in teachers, parents, peers, movies, politicians, and other people in public life. Do you agree with the values your parents taught? Does your experience agree with or contradict what you have been told? Questioning is normal and desirable, and so is some confusion. As you question alternatives and make choices, you are forging your own value system. Your values develop as you experience life.

Attitude and Attitude Change

Have you ever said, "I don't like his attitude?" Or has anyone ever told you, "You should develop a better attitude"? Your attitudes affect how you see other people and what you think their attitudes are. An attitude is made up of your beliefs about something, your feelings about it, and a tendency to behave in a certain way toward the thing. The facts, opinions, and general information you have about the thing are your beliefs. Like, dislike, love, hate, and such emotions are feelings. From the mixture of your beliefs and feelings arises the tendency to behave in the way that expresses the attitude.

For young children, the feeling part of an attitude is probably foremost. They like or dislike what they consider good or bad. Mature people tend to balance feeling with belief. In the family, in school, and with peers, you get formal and informal information that helps shape your attitudes. You learn attitudes through reinforcement—by being rewarded or punished for behavior—and by modeling behavior after others you admire or wish to please.

When the three parts of your attitude don't agree with each

other, you are most open to change. You can change your belief, your feeling, or your behavior. Generally you try to keep
all three in agreement with each other. Suppose you think
cheating is wrong. Then a situation occurs in which you are
convinced that circumstances permit you to cheat on an exam.
Now your behavior is out of line with your belief and feeling.
Something must give, to straighten out the dissonance in your
attitude. You will either reaffirm that you don't believe in
cheating, or change your feelings and beliefs. Or you may try
to justify your act to reduce the discord in your attitude.

Most people resist change. They downgrade the source or
the credibility of the information that calls for change or try to
justify their actions when they behave in contradiction with
their expressed beliefs. If they are publicly committed to an
attitude, they are also less likely to change. Suppose you have
just made a speech favoring an antiabortion bill. You would
not be able to back down from your stand as readily as if your
attitude were unknown. Self-esteem also affects your ability
to change your mind. If your self-confidence is high, you trust
your own judgment more than if you doubt your personal
worth, and so you can accept new information. Reward is
another factor in changing attitudes. For example, people
who are paid to go against their personal attitudes feel less
uncomfortable, less dissonant about their "wrong" behavior
than those not paid to go against their convictions.

A provocative problem of values came up in Kansas City recently. Four minority firemen were offered promotions sooner
than their seniority would normally permit, for the sake of

filling minority quotas. All refused the promotions. A typical remark was, "I have a family, and I always try to tell them right is right, wrong is wrong. I couldn't face my kids if I took the promotion. I would rather have a promotion on merit than to fill a quota." What would you do in their position?

Decisions, Decisions

Without clearly defined values, life seems to lack direction. You have tremendous power over your life. What will you decide to do with it? Will it be wasted? You may say, "Oh, that's an exaggeration. I really have few decisions to make. Somebody else—parents, teachers, the law—calls the shots. I don't get many choices." You actually make dozens of decisions every day. You decided to get out of bed. And to go to school. Did you decide what to eat for breakfast? What to wear? To cheat, or not to cheat, on a math test? Did you choose to take notes in biology class? Did you choose not to speak to a friend you argued with yesterday? Did you argue with your mother about getting your hair cut? Or did you choose to ignore her? Were these conscious or unconscious decisions?

Try to think of five decisions you made today and write them down. Mark a C beside any decision you consider critical. How did you make that choice? Are you proud of or at least pleased with the decisions you made? Or did you act impulsively and do something you now regret?

In many classrooms today students are learning about decision-making processes and how they relate to their values. They begin to see that values are expressed in their actions. When people become aware of what matters to them, they can have more control over their lives. What is important to you? What do you prize or cherish? List ten things you like to do.

Your list may include some of these: reading, watching television, playing the guitar, playing tennis, rapping with friends, hiking, writing poetry, daydreaming, etc. Your list shows your tastes but also something of your values. You may see that you like to be alone more than with other people, or that you prefer your peers to your parents. What things are done alone? Which cost money? What qualities in your life do you prize?

As you move more and more away from your parents you will find that ultimately you have to set your own rules and decide what is right or wrong for you. You can think more objectively about things now than you could as a young child. Your thought is more flexible, and you can see beyond your immediate desires. You can judge an act right, wrong, or in between in terms of intentions and the setting in which it happened. You can "walk in the other man's moccasins" more now than you once could. You begin to understand duty and responsibility, based on reciprocal rights and the expectations people have of each other. A small child thinks of justice in terms of an eye for an eye, a tooth for a tooth, where something wrong must be paid for in terms of punishment meted out from parents or an authority. You can conceive of justice based on making amends for misdeeds, repairing or restoring what has been wronged. Most people wish to behave responsibly and acceptably in their own eyes and the eyes of other people. They care about what is right and wish to do right. As you see more and more of the world in social and moral situations, you absorb what you see, mull it over in your mind, and come to some decisions. You form opinions of yourself in relationship to what you see.

Some of the serious decisions you face as a teen-ager such as how to deal with peer pressures, drinking, sex, marriage, education, and career have long-lasting consequences, and often you must decide pretty much on your own. One psychologist says that the ability to make responsible decisions based on reason and true understanding of one's own values, rather than just drifting into things, is the most valuable skill a teen-ager can develop.

In a class discussion a psychology instructor stated that when people are faced with decisions, they do whatever is easiest. This statement bothered many of the students, who argued vehemently with him. No matter what argument they presented, he shot it down with, "That was the easiest thing to do." Do you think he was right?

By the time you reach the teen years, you have set up some values in your own mind, even though you may not be conscious of them. You have control over many things, and what you decide can make a difference in your life.

Consider these "what if" exercises. What decision is to be made in each case:

► You have a chance to work in a pizza parlor in the summer to help earn money toward college expenses. You could also work as a volunteer in the park system helping with retarded children, which would be related somewhat to your possible career field, special education.

► You are missing a red sweater, and you see it in your friend's closet.

► You know that your best friends are taking liquor from their parent's liquor cabinet. They offer you a drink at a school dance.

► Your friends want you to shoplift. You don't want to but would still like to be friends.

Think of situations where you have been faced with similar choices. Consider all the possible alternatives in each case, even the undesirable ones. What are the consequences of each decision? What would your choice be? Is this what you would honestly do? How do you feel about your decisions? Your decisions give you some insight into your values.

What You Value in Others

What do high-school students value in their peers and in themselves? In a study of 8000 students who were asked how they would like to be remembered in high school, boys said first as an athletic star, then a brilliant student. They ranked being popular last. Girls chose to be a leader in activities, with popularity a close second and scholarship last. Boys said they would rather be a famous athlete than a jet pilot. They ranked atomic scientist and missionary near the bottom of the list. Girls ranked career choices in this order of preference: model, nurse, schoolteacher, and actress.

When asked to judge or reward peers, students consider both moral values and social skills. In the early teens they often give honor to surface values, such as good at games and dancing, socially hep, fun to have around. By seventeen they

outgrow these values as a primary basis for judging personal worth. They no longer respect someone who never gets beyond his early adolescent patterns. They now weight more heavily such values as character, honesty, responsibility, loyalty, kindness, and self-control.

A sophomore English class at Hanford High School in Richland, Washington, had a discussion of values. Steve, fifteen, did a class survey, and came up with these values, rated in order of importance by his peers:

1. Friendship,
   ranked number 1 or 2 by over 50 percent of the class
2. Freedom of choice
3. Comfortable life
4. Family security
5. Salvation
6. Success
7. Mature love
8. National security
9. Grades
10. Social recognition

Steve's list was taken from an eighteen point listing of "terminal" values (goals of life), as developed by Milton Rokeach in his book *The Nature of Human Values*. Here is a composite ranking of Rokeach's values by adult Americans, over twenty-one years old, in late 1968, the most valued being number 1, etc.

	Males	Females
A comfortable life	4	13
An exciting life	18	18
A sense of accomplishment	7	10
A world of peace	1	1
A world of beauty	15	15
Equality	9	8
Family security	2	2
Freedom	3	3
Happiness	5	5
Inner harmony	13	12
Mature love	14	14
National security	10	11
Pleasure	17	16
Salvation	12	4
Self-respect	6	6
Social recognition	16	17
True friendship	11	9
Wisdom	8	7

A Search for Values

Your life is not merely a series of dandelion puffs, blowing away in the breeze and finding a spot of soil in which to root. Each action you perform is a link in the chain that forms your values. Values develop slowly as you begin to find the answer to the question, What do I want out of life? Friends, money, happiness? What makes me happy? How do I choose my own course of action? How do I decide whom to vote for, how to choose a career, how far to go in the back seat of a car on a date, whether to live with someone before marriage?

A friend who teaches behavioral science told me, "Kids want to read self-help articles, just as adults do. They like what they read, but they don't quite know how to put it to use in their own lives."

Human-relations expert Louis Rath developed a values-clarification system that focuses on how you come to hold certain values. Values clarification is a kind of self-audit to help you sort out what has meaning for you. Rath's seven-point valuing system goes like this:

1. Free choice. Without force from anyone, you choose your position.
2. Prize. You cherish the position you take.
3. Evaluate consequences. You weigh and consider advantages and disadvantages.
4. Options. You think about all the options before you choose.
5. Act on or apply your convictions and beliefs.
6. Publicly affirm. Be willing to stand up for your beliefs.
7. Repeatedly and consistently, with a definite pattern of behavior, exhibit a personal commitment to this belief.

As for practical methods you can use, I have included some values-clarification strategies that I hope will help show the way. Some have been given to me by teacher friends, and others are similar to ones developed by Louis Rath, Sidney Simon, and other human-relations experts. Valuing processes are not new. Educators and others working with young people have used similar techniques for years. However, these values-clarification methods are systematic and can help you think through your decision-making processes. Most of the exercises you can do on your own, even though they are well suited for group activity and discussion. Many have been used in communications workshops.

STRATEGY 1: VALUES GRID

Take a sheet of paper and draw a "values grid" like this one:

Issue	1	2	3	4	5	6	7
1.							
2.							
3.							
4.							
5.							
6.							

Think of five or six issues that you feel are important. They could include drinking, trying or using drugs, population control, sex before marriage, etc. After each issue, write a key word or two that summarizes your opinion of it. The seven numbers in the right-hand columns represent these seven questions:

1. Are you proud of your position?
2. Have you publicly affirmed it?
3. Have you chosen from alternatives?
4. Have you given careful consideration of pros and cons and consequences?
5. Did you choose freely?
6. Have you done anything about, acted on, your beliefs?
7. Have you acted consistently, repeatedly?

Ask yourself each of the seven questions about each issue. If you can honestly answer yes, then put a check in the appropriate box. Leave it blank if you cannot answer yes.

The whole point of the values grid is to show that few of our beliefs check out by all seven valuing processes. You need not defend your attitude on any issue. Rather you should evaluate how you arrived at your attitude and how strong your belief is. If you do this analysis in a small group, discuss how your attitude did or did not incorporate the seven points. Remember, a values exercise is not concerned with what your belief is, but is concerned with how you arrived at it.

When you begin to use Rath's seven-point valuing system, it will help you become aware of what you believe now, and it will make you more aware of attitudes in the making in your life. You will begin to weigh the pros and cons of matters for yourself, and you will see when your behavior matches up with what you say you believe. His method lets you see options, so you can make choices and evaluate the actual consequences. In this way, you will develop your own system of values. Every decision you make won't work out well, but as you begin to see the possible choices and how you can control your own life, more and more often the results will satisfy you. When something works well, your self-confidence inches upward. You begin to see that you are putting yourself in charge.

Here are some questions that you may choose from to begin the journey of discovering your values and of finding yourself. Make it a worthwhile trip.

> Do you think there is a serious morality problem in our country?
>
> Do you think that Americans are too competitive?
>
> Do you support the women's liberation movement?
>
> Do you think it's okay to cheat on an income-tax return?
>
> Do you contribute money to any charity?
>
> Do you read any weekly news mazagine?
>
> Do you feel happy when you are alone?
>
> Do you think you would raise your children differently from the way you were raised?
>
> Do you think you would take a job you didn't like if it paid $5000 more per year than a job you did like?
>
> Would you ride home with a friend who was drunk and driving a car?

STRATEGY 2: RANK ORDER

Of the following questions, rank the answers according to your choices. Number 1 is your first choice, etc.

1. Which is most important in a friendship?
   _____ living near each other
   _____ honesty
   _____ loyalty

2. If I gave you $100 what would you do with it?
   _____ buy something for yourself
   _____ give it to charity
   _____ save it

3. If you were president of the United States, what would you give highest priority to?
   _____ energy program
   _____ defense
   _____ poverty

4. Where would you prefer to be on a Saturday afternoon?
   _____ at a shopping center
   _____ at the beach
   _____ in the mountains

5. Which would you like to do least?
   _____ go to a symphony concert
   _____ see a play
   _____ hear a debate

6. In what way do you have the most fun?
   _____ alone
   _____ with a large group

_____ with a few friends

7. Whom would you choose to marry? Someone with

_____ nice personality

_____ sex appeal

_____ intelligence

_____ money

8. Which would you rather have?

_____ trip to Europe

_____ whole new wardrobe

_____ a motorcycle

9. What kind of person would you most want to be?

_____ loving

_____ friendly

_____ intelligent

_____ wealthy

_____ courageous

10. Which is more important in your life?

_____ equality

_____ pleasure

_____ freedom

_____ sense of accomplishment

STRATEGY 3: SOMETHING TO BE PROUD OF

No one is proud of everything he or she thinks or does, but everyone has some things that give him or her pride. Think not of boastful, bragging kinds of feelings but things you feel good about. Choose at least five of the following that you are proud of.

1. Something you have done to resist conformity
2. A family matter
3. Something to do with money
4. Something that had to do with school
5. Something you did to help racial understanding
6. A new skill you have learned in the past year
7. A bad habit you overcame
8. A time that you helped someone when you had nothing to gain from it
9. A situation in which you put your moral beliefs ahead of temptation
10. Something that you can do now that you could not do three years ago.

STRATEGY 4: WHOM TO LEAVE BEHIND

The ten people listed below have been selected as passengers on a spaceship going to another planet. They will be the only survivors when the earth is destroyed tomorrow. A change in space limitations forces the list to be cut to seven passengers. Choose which seven should go. This exercise can also be done in groups of five to ten students. Each group must then unanimously decide which seven go and must decide in thirty minutes. Discuss the choices and how they were made after you complete the exercise.

an accountant

the accountant's pregnant wife

a college girl

a professional baseball player

a female movie star, 30 years old

a black medical student

a famous novelist

a 70-year-old clergyman

a policeman, armed with a gun

   (he and the gun cannot be separated)

a biochemist

How well did you listen to the opinions of others? Were you rigid in your choices? Did you persuade others? You can see that it's hard to determine the best values or any one right value. You may also see that it is difficult to listen to people who believe differently from you. What techniques were used in your group? Is it hard to remain rational when others disagree with you?

STRATEGY 5: WRITE YOUR OWN OBITUARY

By looking at death, people sometimes get a new perspective on life. Here's a sample you can use to fill in the blanks.

John Doe, 16, died yesterday.

He is survived by ———

He was on his way to becoming ———

He always wanted, but never got to ———

He will be remembered for ———

He will be mourned by ——— because ———

The world will suffer the loss of his contributions in the area of ———

In lieu of flowers ———

STRATEGY 6: AN IDEAL DAY

Write about what you would like to do for an ideal twenty-four-hour period. Who would you be with, where would you be, what would you do? Describe the sights, sounds, feelings, smells, weather, anything you fantasize would be part of your ideal day.

STRATEGY 7: INVENTORY

This strategy establishes what the past realities have been in your life and what the present realities are. Do the exercise quickly, keeping each answer brief. If you are working in groups, move quickly from one person to another. If someone chooses not to share, let him pass without criticism or comment. Try not to judge someone's motives.

What has been the happiest period of your life?

What things do you do poorly but must continue doing?

What do you do well?

Tell about a time you missed an opportunity.

What has been your most embarrassing moment?

Tell about a peak experience you have had. Or would like to have.

What has been the lowest point in your life?

Are there some values you are struggling with in your life right now?

What would you like to start doing?

STRATEGY 8: HOW STRONG ARE YOUR BELIEFS?

Using these statements, circle the response that most closely shows how you feel.

SA   Strongly Agree
AS   Agree Somewhat
SD   Strongly Disagree
DS   Disagree Somewhat

The legal age for drinking alcohol should be 18.

   SA   AS   SD   DS

Man is basically good.

   SA   AS   SD   DS

Marijuana should be legalized.

   SA   AS   SD   DS

The United States should pull out of the United Nations.

   SA   AS   SD   DS

Students have little respect for teachers and school.

SA AS SD DS

Adults generally have poor opinions of teen-agers.

SA AS SD DS

Cheating on an exam is sometimes justified.

SA AS SD DS

I am racially prejudiced.

SA AS SD DS

Giving grades encourages the best learning in school.

SA AS SD DS

Ask yourself how you arrived at these decisions. In a group discussion, remember that there is no one correct way to answer. Discussion should help you understand another person's point of view and to accept that person's right to feel different from the way you do.

STRATEGY 9

Rank the following occupations in order of prestige, the most prestigious having number 1, etc.

Novelist
Newspaper columnist
Policeman
Lawyer
Sociologist
Public-school teacher
Scientist
Judge

Actor

Dentist

Engineer

Physician

College professor

Banker

Real-estate broker

Politician

Psychologist

STRATEGY 10: ADJECTIVES THAT DESCRIBE YOU

List twenty adjectives that best describe you. Put a check by all those you consider of great importance. Now take your list and divide it into positive, negative, and neutral adjectives.

STRATEGY 11

Which five of the following characteristics are most important for a community leader? Put them in ranking order.

interested in people

well organized

energetic

emotionally stable

intelligent

loyal to community

special experience

sense of humor

respected in community
good in social situations
broad general experience
financially independent
knowledgeable about local issues
politically aware
shows initiative
good health

STRATEGY 12

These questions should be answered Yes, No, or Maybe.
They will help you see more carefully what you would like
to become and to consider what things you value. Are you
someone who . . .

would rather have a car than go to Europe?
only wants two children?
wishes you had different parents?
would not allow your hair to show its gray?
would be troubled if a member of another ethnic group
   moved into your neighborhood?
definitely wants to move away from your hometown?
will someday run for public office?
would likely publish a short story?
would invite someone of a different race to your home for
   dinner?
will often write letters to the newspaper editor?
wants a house in the suburbs?

would marry someone of a different religion?

would be active in civil-rights causes?

would hate a big wedding?

can't have fun unless you are with the opposite sex?

will probably marry more than once?

will probably marry before you are twenty-one?

will make a good mother or father?

would be very unhappy if you did not have a television set?

Now think about your answers. Add ten more questions of your own. If you are in a group, share one question that you have given a very definite answer to. If you care to, tell the group why you felt that way.

STRATEGY 13: SOME SPECIFIC WHAT IFS

What would you do if . . .

you had three wishes?

you had a million dollars?

you could choose one person to live on an island with you?

you had twenty-four hours to live?

Write a few sentences, or a whole page, about each question. Date your answers, and put the page aside in a favorite book, somewhere safe. Make a note on your calendar to take it out and read it one year from now.

Here are two paragraphs written by students who were asked what they would do if they had twenty-four hours to live.

Debbie, seventeen, wrote, "I would have to think about

what was important to me. I would get up early, watch the sunrise. Then I'd hurry around to finish all the jobs I had left lying around. I would spend the last hours with my parents, and I would talk with them about my life. Sometimes I feel guilty not doing enough with my life. I want to be stable and sound. I don't want to be rejected by people, by friends, by society. I want the strength to learn who I am, to start to think on my own."

Jonathan, fifteen, wrote, "I would go as far as I could from town, race my motorcycle at the fastest speed I could, try everything I could as fast as possible. I would run through Macy's and grab the most expensive things in sight. I would go on a hilltop and scream. I would hug my girl friend. I would be angry. I might cry."

The goal of all these value-finding strategies is to involve you in practical experiences that may help you become aware of your own feelings. The choices you make should be deliberate ones. You can also use these strategies to devise more of your own.

If you have tried some of the strategies, you have probably discovered that some of your opinions or ideas come quickly without much hard, long thought. Many people find that life experiences "just happen." They didn't plan for things to go that way, but here they are. Well, why not have more to say about what happens in your life? Put yourself in charge. Think through the things you believe.

CHAPTER EIGHT

Finding Your Own Way

The future is always in some respects,
for better or for worse, different from the past.
S. HAYAKAWA

Within the limits of reality and your own ability, you can do whatever you want with your life. Think back to a day when you truly felt good. At the end of the day, you had a warm glow. You may have thought, "That was a good day. I got a lot done. I like the way things went today." You felt a sense of accomplishment. In contrast, think of a day when things weren't so great. You seemed to rub everybody the wrong way, and

145

you couldn't feel pleased with anything or anyone. What went wrong? What did you do to cause that feeling? We all have both kinds of days, and a lot that are in between. The more times you can ask, "What from within me caused that?" the more you begin to know yourself. Ask yourself this question when it's a good day as well as when it's a bad one. Take a long look within. Much hate is self-hate. How can people accept flaws in others if they never learn to accept their own? Is someone wrong because he is different from us?

No one wants to stay a child. Everyone wants to grow up. Everyone wants to be big, to have power. Is everything you do just trying to be big? Do you grow in the direction you desire, or is growth haphazard?

What are your plans? Take stock of what you have in mind for yourself for the future, tomorrow, five years from now. One student of mine in a writing class wrote of his future: "I see myself in a long tunnel, like a giant sewer pipe, and I'm sliding, sliding from one side to another. The tunnel goes on and on, and I can't stop from falling into nothing."

Another wrote, "My future is a deserted house."

Another said, "I want to know what makes me tick."

Goals and Priorities

Katie, fourteen, wrote, "There are so many millions of things out there to do in the world, so many that I want to try, that I don't know where to begin, so I do nothing."

You may be caught in that frustration, too. How many of those millions of things are important? Try this ten-minute self-exam similar to one developed by Alan Lakein, time-management specialist. Set a timer for ten minutes. As fast as you can, write down what your lifetime goals are. How would you like to spend the next five years? Then write down your goal for the next six months. Choose three of your long-range goals to spend time on during the next seven days. The answers are for your own use, so don't worry about putting in things other people might like to hear. Leave space to go back and add a few more things.

Set up a sheet of paper for each goal you can spend time on during the next week. You have 168 hours in each week. Write down all the things you can do to move toward your goal. Make the longest possible list in your allotted ten minutes. Now go back and draw a line through every item you don't actually intend to do. Decide what is the single most important item on your list. It is your A priority item. If you wish, you can also identify B and C priorities. Then start doing A.

You can toss all your sheets in the wastebasket if you want to, but you can also begin to bring some reality to vague dreams and notions. A lot of people won't put their goals down on paper because they're afraid to see them.

Suppose your six-month goals read: Some new friends, better grades, start guitar lessons. What can you do to move toward those goals? Maybe a lifetime goal is "to be happy." You must have a long list of things you can do toward that goal. Or do you?

Here's another method you can use to see how you spend your time. Draw a large circle and divide it into four quarters using dotted lines. Each quarter represents six hours of the day. Now estimate how many hours or fractions of an hour you spend during a normal school day on sleep, school, with friends, with family—including meals—alone, on a job that earns money, chores, or homework, on miscellaneous other things. Draw slices in your "pie of life" to show how you use your time. What do you think about your slices of life? Are you satisfied with how your time is being spent? If not, draw what you feel would be an ideal pie. Is there a realistic way you can change your actual times to meet your ideal ones? Sort out your pie slices and mark each one *I* for important, *NI* for not important. Mark them also *D* for dull and *I* for interesting.

You are developing goals and values now as you move about in your expanding world, and many things compete for your time. You need to feel a sense of autonomy, that you are indeed in charge of your life. You look for things worthy of commitment. Setting some goals for yourself can help you sort out priorities. You'll begin to make some sense out of the maze of many things to do, and you'll learn to make time for what is important to you. You won't be pulled in so many directions once you have thought about your goals.

People absorb the standards that are valued in their culture. Parents seem to socialize a child for life as they themselves know it. The working-class child may put more value on security, see more sharply defined sex roles, place less value on education than a middle-class child. On the other hand, he may be expected to support himself and contribute to the family sooner than the middle-class child. Clearly the middle-class child gets a break in educational opportunity and has more chance to discover possible ways of self-improvement. The less-advantaged child probably has more opportunity to break out of the mold than ever before, but when he does seek another role, he has to work a lot harder at it than the advantaged child.

Whatever your economic background, a wide variety of options is open to you in adolescence. When you make a specific choice of which track to follow, the expectations that are held for a person who makes that choice become an important force in your development. "I plan to be a research biologist," one student says. Another says, "I'm going to be a plumber." Another, "I'm going to be a secretary." Another, "I'm going to get a job somewhere and buy a Porsche." For each of these people, you expect different things.

Your occupation is a significant definer of roles. You have a sense of self-identity through your chosen field. A good choice means that you have found the right fit to your talents and ability that satisfies your needs. Today many occupations have been glamorized on television and in the movies. Occupations have been highly embellished with the fantasy and drama of peak moments. In reality you may find them dull and stale by comparison to what you have been shown. I recall a summer recently spent on jury duty. I was a juror for a stabbing case, a paternity suit, and a murder trial. There was no resemblance between them and Perry Mason cases.

A study of characteristics for many occupations found that images were not accurate, although the 1000 students who participated agreed on characteristics for each occupation. Medicine was thought to be a glamorous career, and the doctor should be stable, responsible, confident. A teacher was ranked low in influence, status, wealth. A lawyer was defined as self-assertive and a manipulator. Such stereotypes can mislead you when you think of matching your interests with a career.

In a rap session, high-school seniors were discussing values and goals. The day was a downer for Mike, and he said, "Yeah, we're all in the same rat race, for grades, getting an education, then for a job, another rat race. You work, you live, you die. All about the same, and somebody else pulls the strings on most things."

Someone asked him, "Do you think you have so little control over what you do?"

"Well," he argued, "there are certain things I can't do because I'm still dependent on my parents. A lot of things are dictated to me by them—or by money. I wish I knew what all the hard work of a college degree would lead to. I wish I knew the one and only right job for me."

For a student planning on a career in engineering, Mike showed little enthusiasm and a great deal of anxiety. Are your chosen goals the right ones for you? The venture into any career field is a venture into the unknown. Don't worry about the "one and only right job" for you. You should plan—in line with your interests, likes, and abilities—to take courses that fit your future goals. They will likely lead to several career possibilities.

Sometimes the appeal of a career may be in what it does not require rather than what it does. If you wish to deal with people and feel a strong need to achieve, then you would reject passive jobs. If you want to be totally absorbed in your work, uninterrupted by other people, you would choose another kind of work. The amount and variety of social stimulation in a job can be an important factor in its satisfaction for you.

While needs for achievement vary tremendously, most people look for a sense of satisfaction from their work. The satisfaction may be in getting a fat paycheck to buy a fancy car and other material things, and this accomplishment may meet the needs of one person very nicely. Everyone has heard the saying, "Money can't buy happiness." Humorist Art Buchwald had a quick retort: "I hear you, but I'd sure like to find out for myself, rather than always having to take someone else's word for it." A well-paying job is more important to some people than to others. Nevertheless, the money earned on the job should not be the only or prime consideration to determine your career choices.

Maturity

In the rapidly changing culture of the United States today, each person must learn to rely more on himself to deal with continual change. One in five American families moves from one house to another each year. The move is often geographically distant from friends and relatives. In order to cope with new experiences people need to develop a strong personal code of behavior. They should be in full charge of themselves as they move toward maturity.

Here's what other teen-agers have written about maturity and independence, their hopes and dreams. They were asked, "Have you earned some adult privileges? Do you handle situations any differently from the way you did three years ago? What are your inner thoughts, your dreams and goals?"

Carla: Last summer my parents went away for a week. My brother and I stayed home on our own. When they came home, everything was in good shape. We never did anything we couldn't be proud of.

Rich: I have my driver's license now and a weekend job. I earn my own gas money and car-insurance money, so I feel good about having car privileges and carrying some of the weight.

Jane: We had a rough year. My dad was out of work, my mother was in the hospital. I wanted to sit down and cry, things were so bad. But I took care of the house, visited my mother, helped out with my little sister, and we all made it through a bad time. In the end my dad said how proud he was of me, and I was glad I didn't fall apart.

David: Three years ago I did whatever the crowd did. They drank. I drank. They lifted [shoplifted]. I lifted. I was making a wreck of myself, and I didn't like me too much. Now I'm in better shape. I can handle peer pressure. My grades show it, too.

Other comments were:

I may never come to fame and fortune, but this won't matter as long as I'm happy. I want to know that I'm loved and to love back. Little things, smiles, being with people, this can make me happy.

The most important thing I dream of is finding love and not being laughed at.

I have no great desire for material things, although I don't mind having them.

Death doesn't frighten me. Life does. Will I, only one small person, be able to make my life worth living?

These thoughts are from your own generation. The dreams are there. Will they become reality? Who will you be? Who's in charge here? Ultimately you are in charge of your own life forces. You must answer to yourself for the outcome of today and for the outcome of your future. If you want something, go after it. In the year A.D. 60, Epictetus said, "First say to yourself, what would you be; and then do what you have to do." Use your own initiative, every resource you can find.

You will surely find disappointments in life, when things

can't be the way you would like them to be. What other people say and do will always affect you. You may not be elected class president or invited to join something. Someone else may get the job you wanted. The disappointments themselves are not the important matters. It's how you handle them that counts.

You affect the world around you, just as it affects you. Some things you can change when you don't like them and others you have to live with. You can walk away from people and situations that don't bring out the best in you. You have it within you to seek people and situations that do bring out your best qualities. In the teen years you have a new beginning, a challenge to grow, to learn who you are and who you can be.

The more you know about yourself, the better you will understand other people. How is it with you? What's going on in your life? Know yourself, and you'll have a realistic chance of being all that you can be.

Bibliography

Adams, J. F., "Adolescent Personal Problems as a Function of Age and Sex." *Journal of Genetic Psychology,* Vol. 104 (June, 1964), pp. 207-214.

Branden, Nathaniel, *The Psychology of Self-Esteem.* Los Angeles: Nash Publishing Corporation, 1969.

Coleman, James S., *The Adolescent Society.* New York: The Free Press of Glencoe, Inc., 1961.

Coopersmith, Stanley, *The Antecedents of Self-Esteem.* San Francisco: W. H. Freeman & Company, 1967.

Erikson, Erik H., *Identity: Youth and Crisis.* New York: W. W. Norton & Company, Inc., 1968.

Ginott, Haim G., *Between Parent and Teenager.* New York: The Macmillan Company, 1969.

Hayakawa, S. I., *Symbol, Status, and Personality.* New York: Harcourt, Brace & World, Inc., 1963.

Johnson, Eric W., *Sex: Telling It Straight*. Philadelphia: J. B. Lippincott Company, 1970.

Lair, Jess, *I Ain't Much, Baby—But I'm All I've Got*. New York: Doubleday & Company, Inc., 1972.

Maslow, Abraham H., *Motivation and Personality*. New York: Harper & Bros., 1954.

Rogers, Carl R., *On Becoming a Person*. Boston: Houghton Mifflin Company, 1961.

Rosenberg, Morris, *Society and the Adolescent Self-Image*. Princeton: Princeton University Press, 1965.

Strommen, Merton P., *Five Cries of Youth*. New York: Harper & Row, Publishers, 1974.

Index